KETO DIET

BOOK

FOR BEGINNERS UK 2023

180 Weight Loss And Low Carb Recipe Cookbook For
Healthy living Incl 4 weeks Meal Plan

Daniel A. Wolford

Disclaimer

The sole aim of this book is to educate. It is important to consult
your dietician as individual body may vary, contents in this book
a generally for educative purpose, The author is not responsible
for any damage directly or indirectly caused by the information
contained in this book

Content

Introduction

The ketogenic diet, popularly known as the "keto diet," is a high-fat, low-carbohydrate eating plan that compels the body to use fat as fuel rather than carbs. It was initially created in the 1920s as a treatment for epilepsy, but research has since revealed that it also offers a variety of other health advantages, such as the ability to lose weight, improve blood sugar regulation, and lower the chance of developing heart disease.

The early 1900s saw the beginning of research into the impact of fasting on epilepsy, which is when the ketogenic diet got its start. They discovered that for certain individuals, fasting could assist to lessen the frequency and severity of seizures. Fasting was not a viable long-term treatment, so scientists started looking for ways to simulate its benefits without having patients to abstain from meals.

The first ketogenic diet was created by Dr. Russell Wilder, a medical professional at the Mayo Clinic, in 1921. This diet was created to force the body to burn fat for energy while yet giving it enough calories to maintain weight. The epilepsy diet was initially effective in treating the condition, and for many years it was the go-to therapy.

The emergence of new anti-epileptic drugs in the 1950s, however, led to a fall in the keto diet's appeal. Many people converted to these drugs because they were more convenient to use and more efficient than the keto diet.

The keto diet has gained appeal as a weight-loss and health-improving diet in recent years. This is partly because more and more studies are proving its advantages. According to studies, the ketogenic diet can lower heart disease risk, help people lose weight, and improve blood sugar regulation.

But there are hazards associated with the ketogenic diet. It may result in negative side effects like weariness, nauseousness, and constipation. Before beginning the keto diet, it's vital to consult your doctor, especially if you have any underlying medical issues.

Here are some significant occasions in the background of the ketogenic diet

1911: French researchers publish a study demonstrating that fasting can help epileptic sufferers experience fewer seizures. At the Mayo Clinic, Dr. Russell Wilder creates the first ketogenic diet in 1921.

The ketogenic diet becomes the go-to method of treating epilepsy in the 1920s. 1950s: As new anti-epileptic drugs are developed, the popularity of the ketogenic diet falls.

1990s: The keto diet reemerges as a popular weight-loss plan.

2010s: Millions of individuals adopt the keto diet as a popular eating plan.

Despite being a relatively recent diet, the keto diet has a lengthy and fascinating history. It has been used to treat epilepsy for more than a century, and it is currently being researched for possible advantages in the treatment of other disorders like weight loss and heart health.

Chapter 1

Keto Diet

The Ketogenic Diet, sometimes known as the Keto Diet, is a low-carb, high-fat eating plan that has become well-known for its potential to aid in weight loss and improve a number of medical issues. The core idea behind the Keto diet is to switch the body's metabolism from using glucose (sugar) as its main source of energy to using ketones, which are formed by the liver's breakdown of lipids. Ketosis is the name given to this metabolic condition.

About 70–75% of calories on the Keto diet are typically derived from fat, 20–25% from protein, and only 5–10% from carbohydrates. Compared to the typical Western diet, which is high in carbohydrates, this is a considerable change.

How Does Keto Diet Work?

Your body begins to run low on glucose, which it typically uses for energy, when you dramatically reduce your carbohydrate intake. In reaction, the liver starts to break down fats into ketones, a different type of fuel. The body's cells, particularly those in the brain, use these ketones as fuel.

Benefits of a Keto diet include

1. Losing weight : The Keto Diet's potential to promote weight loss is one of the main reasons people use it. The low-carb diet's ability to regulate insulin levels can result in decreased fat storage and enhanced fat burning.

2. Blood Sugar that Is Stable: Dietary restrictions on carbohydrates can help to normalize blood sugar levels. For people with type 2 diabetes or those who are at risk of developing it, this might be helpful.

3. Improved Mental Focus: Some people believe that a ketosis-induced increase in mental clarity and focus. Ketones are an effective energy source for the brain.

4. Increased Energy: Many people report having more energy throughout the day as their bodies get used to using ketones as fuel.

5. Appetite Suppression: The diet's high fat and moderate protein composition will help you feel satiated and full longer, which may help you resist the urge to overeat.

6. Epilepsy Therapy: The Keto diet was first created in the 1920s as a method of treating epilepsy, especially in kids who didn't respond to medication. It is still employed occasionally today.

7. Potential Advantages for Heart Health According to several studies, the Keto diet may reduce triglyceride levels and raise HDL cholesterol levels, two risk factors for heart disease. More study is, however, required in this field.

Foods to Eat While on the Keto Diet Include

Avocado, almonds, seeds, olive oil, coconut oil, butter, and fatty seafood like salmon are examples of "Healthy Fats".

Proteins : Meat, poultry, fish, eggs, and dairy products, ideally those with a high fat content like cheese and Greek yogurt.

Leafy greens, broccoli, cauliflower, zucchini, peppers, and other non-starchy vegetables.

Berries: Berries such as strawberries, raspberries, and blackberries can be used sparingly.

Snacks: Low-carb snacks, cheese, nuts, and seeds.

<u>Avoid these foods</u>

Bread, pasta, rice, potatoes, sweet snacks, and sugary drinks are examples of high-carb foods.

Fruits that are heavy in sugar, such as bananas, grapes, oranges, and other similar fruits.

Processed foods include: Foods that have been highly processed and packaged frequently have hidden carbs.

A few vegetables Due to their increased carb content, starchy vegetables like maize and peas should be consumed in moderation.

Sugar and Sweeteners: Steer clear of all artificial sweeteners and sugar in any form.

Grains and legumes Beans, lentils, and chickpeas are very heavy in carbohydrates.

Potential Drawbacks and Factors to Take into Account

1. Keto Flu: When starting the Keto diet, some people experience flu-like symptoms. The symptoms of what is frequently referred to as the "keto flu" include weariness, headache, dizziness, and irritability. The body has adjusted to using fat for fuel, which is the cause of it.

2. Nutritional Deficits: A diet that is too restrictive can result in vitamin and mineral deficiencies. You should carefully plan your meals to make sure you're getting enough nutrition.

3. Digestive Problems Some persons may experience diarrhea and constipation as a result of the abrupt increase in dietary lipids.

4. Social Challenges As many items are forbidden on the Keto Diet, it might be challenging to follow it when out with friends or eating at restaurants.

5. Long-Term Safety: Although short-term study points to possible advantages, there is still much to learn about the long-term security and

durability of the ketogenic diet.

It's crucial to speak with a healthcare provider or certified nutritionist before beginning any new diet, including the Keto Diet, especially if you have underlying medical issues. They may offer advice on how to follow the diet safely and successfully as well as assist you in determining whether it is suitable for your particular needs.

Chapter 2

Grocery Lists for a keto diet

Leafy greens (spinach, kale, collard greens, arugula) as well as broccoli,

cauliflower

asparagus,

Brussels sprouts,

cucumbers,

avocados,

tomatoes,

zucchini,

eggplant,

mushrooms,

onions, and peppers.

Dairy

Full-fat cheese,

heavy cream,

butter,

ghee,

sour cream,

yogurt, and cottage cheese.

Bakery products

Baking powder,

baking soda,

psyllium husk powder,

erythritol,

monk fruit,

almond,

coconut, and stevia flour.

Condiments

Olive oil,

avocado oil,

coconut oil,

vinegar (balsamic, apple cider, red wine),

hot sauce,

mustard,

salt,

pepper, and other herbs and spices (paprika, cumin, chili powder, garlic powder, onion powder).

Meat

Fish

Seafood

Beef

Lamb

Pork

Chicken

Turkey.

Seasoning and herbs

Cumin,

chili powder,

oregano,

thyme,

rosemary,

basil,

garlic powder,

onion powder,

paprika.

Poultry

Turkey

Chicken

Other

Nut butters (peanut butter, almond butter, cashew butter),

seeds, and nuts (almonds, walnuts, pecans, chia seeds, hemp seeds)

 Whey protein

(Collagen powder)

Bone broth

<u>Here are some more pointers for adhering to the ketogenic diet</u>

To make sure you're receiving the appropriate balance, start by keeping track of your macronutrients (carbohydrates, protein, and fat).

Aim for 20 to 30 grams of net carbohydrates per day.

Consume lots of protein and good fats.

Drink plenty of water and other low-carb beverages to stay hydrated. Give your body time to become used to the keto diet by being patient.

Chapter 3

Essential Foods on a Keto Diet

<u>1-3. Animal proteins</u>

<u>1. Seafood</u>

Fish and shellfish are excellent keto food choices. Along with being practically carb-free, salmon and other fish are also high in selenium, potassium, and B vitamins.

But different types of shellfish have different carbohydrate counts. Oysters and octopus contain carbohydrates, however shrimp and the majority of crabs don't. On the keto diet, you can still eat these things, but you must carefully monitor your carb intake to keep inside your target range.

Omega-3 fats, which are abundant in salmon, sardines, mackerel, and other fatty fish, have also been linked to lower insulin levels and higher insulin sensitivity in overweight or obese adults.

2. Poultry and meat

On the ketogenic diet, meat and poultry are regarded as staple foods.

Fresh meat and poultry are low in carbohydrates and high in B vitamins as well as other vital minerals. Additionally, they're a fantastic source of high-quality protein, which may aid in maintaining muscle mass while following a very low-carb diet.

Given that it contains more omega-3 fats and conjugated linoleic acid (CLA) than meat from grain-fed animals, it may be advisable to pick grass-fed beef, if at all possible.

3. Eggs

Eggs are a very nutritious source of protein.

Eggs can be a great keto food because they have roughly 6 grams of protein and less than 1 gram of carbohydrates per large egg.

Eggs have also been demonstrated to release chemicals that heighten feelings of satiety.

The majority of an egg's nutrients are found in the yolk, thus it's crucial to consume whole eggs rather than egg whites. This includes the eye-health preserving antioxidants lutein and zeaxanthin.

Despite having a lot of cholesterol, egg yolks don't seem to make you more likely to develop heart disease.

The majority of animal proteins, including beef, pork, chicken, eggs, and shellfish, are low in carbohydrates and suitable for the keto diet.

4-7. Dairy products and dairy substitutes

4. Cheese

There are several varieties of cheese, the most of which are high in fat and very low in carbohydrates, making them ideal for the keto diet.

One gram of carbohydrates, six grams of protein, and a healthy dose of calcium are all present in only one ounce (28 grams) of cheddar cheese.

Despite having a lot of saturated fat, cheese hasn't been proven to make you more likely to get heart disease.

Additionally, cheese includes CLA, which has been connected to benefits in body composition and fat loss.

Additionally, frequent cheese consumption may lessen the aging-related loss of muscular mass and strength.

These cheeses have fewer carbohydrates and are suitable for a ketogenic diet.

Blue cheese keto cheese list

Camembert, Brie, cheddar, and chevre

Cottage cheese and cream cheese with colby jack

feta

a goat cheese

halloumi

Havarti

Limburger

Mascarpone Manchego

mozzarella

Muenster

Provolone pepper jack parmesan

string cheese romano

French cheese

5. Greek yogurt and cottage cheese

Cottage cheese and plain Greek yogurt are healthy, high-protein foods. You can eat them in moderation when on keto even if they do contain some carbs.

Yogurt and cottage cheese have both been demonstrated to aid in reducing hunger and fostering feelings of fullness.

Both of these are delicious on their own as a snack, but you can also mix them with chopped almonds, cinnamon, or other spices to create a quick keto treat.

6. cream and half-and-half

The fatty part of fresh milk that is removed during milk processing makes up cream. On the other hand, half-and-half is a mixture of half whole milk

and half cream.

These two dairy products are both excellent for keto because they are both very low in carbohydrates and high in fat.

Butter and cream are high in CLA like other fatty dairy products, which may help with fat loss.

Despite this, it is preferable to only sometimes indulge in cream and half-and-half.

Popular choices for adding to coffee or substituting for tiny amounts of milk when cooking on the keto diet are cream and half-and-half.

7. Milk made from plants without sugar

Soy, almond, and coconut milk are among the plant-based milk variants that are suitable for the keto diet.

You ought to pick versions without added sugar. Options that have been sweetened contain too much sugar to be deemed keto-friendly.

Furthermore, you should stay away from oat milk because even unsweetened oat milk has too many carbs to be suitable for a ketogenic

diet.

Keto-friendly dairy and dairy substitutes include cheese, plain yogurt, cottage cheese, cream, half-and-half, and some unsweetened plant milks.

<u>8–12. Veggies</u>

<u>8. Vegetables with green leaves</u>

Green leafy vegetables are ideal for the keto diet since they have a very low carb count. They are also abundant sources of antioxidants, minerals, and vitamins.

Dark leafy greens, in particular, such as spinach, kale, and collard greens, are abundant in iron and vitamin K.

Greens provide your meals more substance without significantly raising the carbohydrate content. In addition, herbs like oregano and rosemary give substantial flavor with hardly any carbohydrates.

These leafy greens are suitable for keto diets.

lettuce, baby spinach, arugula, escarole, and frisee are among the salad greens.

Greens for cooking include kale, spinach, Swiss chard, bok choy, collard

greens, and cabbage.

herbs such as rosemary, thyme, sage, mint, oregano, dill, parsley, cilantro, and lemongrass

9. Peppers

There are numerous types of peppers, and they are all acceptable for the keto diet. Despite the fact that they are essentially fruits, they are cooked like vegetables.

Jalapenos are excellent for crafting keto-friendly appetizers since they are small fiery peppers that add flavor to recipes. Larger, milder peppers, such as bell peppers and poblanos, can be stuffed to create excellent, low-carb main courses.

Additionally, peppers contain a lot of vitamin C. One bell pepper, for instance, has 107% of the recommended daily intake (RDI) of vitamin C.

10. Squash in summer

Yellow squash and zucchini are two summer squashes that are low in carbohydrates and quite adaptable.

In fact, zucchini is a staple of the keto diet. You can make zucchini noodles with a spiralizer, which are a great alternative to pasta or noodles.

Grated zucchini can be used to replace rice or added to baked products without changing their flavor. It can also be prepared as a cold salad by slicing it thinly with a mandoline and tossing it with salt, pepper, and olive oil.

11. fatty vegetables

Although technically both fruits, avocados and olives stand out among vegetables because of their relatively high fat content. They are also fiber-rich and have few net carbohydrates.

The primary antioxidant in olives, oleuropein, has anti-inflammatory qualities and might save your cells from oxidative stress.

12. Additional no starchy vegetables.

Other non-starchy veggies are high in minerals and antioxidants while being low in calories and carbohydrates.

Furthermore, low-carb vegetables are excellent alternatives to diets high in carbohydrates.

For instance, making cauliflower rice or mashed cauliflower using low carb cauliflower is simple. A fantastic natural substitution for spaghetti is spaghetti squash, and low-carb root vegetables like jicama and turnips work well in place of roasted potatoes or french fries.

Here are some other instances of veggies that are suitable for the keto diet.

veggie list for keto

asparagus

cauliflower cabbage

Caucasian mushrooms

Cucumber, beans, eggplant, and tomatoes

Jicama, spaghetti squash, radishes, and turnips

Belgian spuds

Celiac Okra

vegetables to stay away from when following the keto diet

Not all vegetables are low in carbohydrates, so keep that in mind. Some foods should be avoided when following a ketogenic diet, including as potatoes, sweet potatoes, onions (in excessive quantities), some winter squashes, such as acorn squash and butternut squash, corn, and others.

On the keto diet, you should consume a lot of nonstarchy vegetables, such as leafy greens, summer squash, peppers, avocados, and olives.

13-16. Additional vegan food

13. Seeds and nuts

Nuts and seeds have a high fat content and few carbohydrates.

The risk of heart disease, several malignancies, depression, and other chronic disorders is connected to frequent nut consumption.

Additionally, nuts and seeds have a lot of fiber, which can make you feel full and help you consume less calories.

The amount of net carbohydrates varies greatly by variety of nut and seed, despite the fact that most are low. The foods with the fewest carbohydrates are those that are excellent for keto.

Macadamia and almond nuts

pecans

walnuts

the chia seed

flaxseeds

14. Berries

 Berry consumption is an exception to the rule that most fruits contain too many carbohydrates for keto dieters.

Berries are low in carbohydrates and high in fiber, especially strawberries and raspberries. Despite having fewer carbohydrates than some other fruits, blackberries and blueberries might not be suitable for stringent keto diets.

Antioxidants included in these little fruits may aid to decrease inflammation and provide disease protection.

15. Shirataki noodles

The keto diet is a great fit for shirataki noodles. Because they are mainly water, they provide only 15 calories and less than 1 gram of net carbohydrates per serving.

These noodles are constructed of glucomannan, a viscous fiber with numerous potential health advantages.

The gel-like consistency of viscous fiber delays the passage of food through your digestive system. This may facilitate weight loss and diabetes control by reducing hunger and blood sugar rises.

There are many different types of shirataki noodles, such as rice, fettuccine, and linguine. They may virtually all be substituted for ordinary noodles in recipes.

16. Cocoa powder and dark chocolate

Antioxidants can be found in dark chocolate and cocoa.

Flavanols included in dark chocolate may minimize your risk of heart disease by decreasing blood pressure and maintaining the health of your arteries.

Surprisingly, you can have chocolate while on the keto diet. But it's crucial to select dark chocolate that has at least 70% cocoa solids, preferably more, and to consume it in moderation.

Berries, shirataki noodles, almonds, seeds, and dark chocolate are additional plant foods that are excellent for keto diets.

Oils and fats

17. Olive oil

Olive oil has remarkable heart-health advantages.

It contains a lot of oleic acid, a monounsaturated fat that has been shown to lower risk factors for heart disease.

Extra-virgin olive oil is also rich in polyphenol antioxidants, which are plant substances that preserve heart health further by reducing inflammation and enhancing arterial function.

Olive oil is a pure fat source; it is devoid of carbohydrates. It makes a great base for healthy mayonnaise and salad dressings.

It's preferable to use olive oil for low heat cooking or to add it to meals after they've been cooked because it doesn't maintain its stability at high temperatures as well as saturated fats do.

Coconut oil and avocado oil are some fantastic plant-based oils to test when on a ketogenic diet.

18. Ghee and butter

Good fats to include on the keto diet are butter and ghee. Ghee is completely free of carbohydrates, while butter has very little amounts.

Clarified butter, or ghee, is created by heating butter and skimming off the milk particles that float to the top. It is frequently used in Indian cooking and has a rich buttery flavor.

Butter and ghee, like other full-fat dairy products, don't seem to be as bad for your health as previously believed.

Olive oil, butter, and ghee are the greatest fats and oils for keto cooking and baking. Additionally excellent options include avocado and coconut oils.

19–20. Drinks

19. Coffee and tea without sugar

Tea and coffee are nutritious, carb-free beverages.

They contain caffeine, which speeds up your metabolism and could enhance your mood, mental clarity, and physical stamina.

Additionally, it has been demonstrated that coffee and tea consumers have a much lower chance of developing diabetes. Though a cause and effect connection has not yet been established, people who drink the most coffee actually have the lowest risk.

You can add heavy cream to coffee or tea; but, since "light" lattes are often manufactured with nonfat milk and high-carb flavorings, you must stay away from them while on the ketogenic diet.

20. Unsweetened Sparkling water

Unsweetened sparkling water is a fantastic soda substitute for people on the keto diet.

These deliciously bubbly drinks may have flavors, but they usually don't include any sugar or sweeteners. They are hence devoid of calories and carbohydrates.

However, certain kinds naturally flavor themselves with trace amounts of fruit juice, and these could be carb-rich. Check the label carefully because extra carbs can add up rapidly.

Sparkling water, unsweetened tea, and coffee are all suitable keto drinks.

Chapter 4

<u>4 Week Meal Plan</u>

<u>Week 1</u>

<u>Day 1</u>

- Breakfast: Keto Sausage Breakfast Sandwich

- Lunch: Zucchini Pasta with Creamy Avocado Pesto

- Dinner: Salmon with Creamy Dill Sauce

Day 2

- Breakfast: Keto Cloud Eggs

- Lunch: Greek Chicken Salad

- Dinner: Cheese and Spinach Stuffed Chicken

Day 3

- Breakfast: Keto Breakfast Casserole

- Lunch: Keto Cobb Salad

- Dinner: Avocado & Basil Salmon

Day 4

- Breakfast: Keto Cinnamon Roll Knots

- Lunch: Keto Tuna Salad

- Dinner: Walnut Crusted Salmon

Day 5

- Breakfast: Keto Zucchini Bread

- Lunch: Antipasto Salad

- Dinner: Keto Chicken Enchilada Bowl

Day 6

- Breakfast: Low Carb Bacon and Cheese Scones

- Lunch: Keto Spinach Salad with Feta and Walnuts

- Dinner: Buffalo Chicken Soup

Day 7

- Breakfast: Keto Burrito

- Lunch: Keto Arugula Salad with Halloumi and Balsamic Dressing

- Dinner: Sheet Pan Chicken and Rainbow Veggies

Day 8

- Breakfast: Popper Egg Cups

- Lunch: Keto Zucchini Salad with Ranch Dressing

- Dinner: Salmon With Bacon & Tomato Cream Sauce

Day 9

- Breakfast: Avocado Toast with Eggs

- Lunch: Keto Vegetarian Meatballs

- Dinner: Salmon & Asparagus Foil Packs

Day 10

- Breakfast: Keto Waffles

- Lunch: Low Carb Mediterranean Quesadillas

- Dinner: Creamy Tuscan Chicken

Day 11

- Breakfast: Keto Smoothie

- Lunch: Veggie Tacos

- Dinner: Cheese and pepperoni chips (as a snack) + Keto Eggplant Parmesan

Day 12

- Breakfast: Spinach Stuffed Mushroom

- Lunch: Crispy Tofu and Bok Choy Salad

- Dinner: Salmon Stuffed Avocado

Day 13

- Breakfast: Zucchini nacho chips

- Lunch: Guacamole with cucumber slices

- Dinner: Keto Salmon Cakes

Day 14

- Breakfast: Deviled eggs with bacon

- Lunch: Easy Keto Stuffed Eggplant

- Dinner: Avocado & Basil Salmon

<u>Week 3</u>

<u>Day 15</u>

- Breakfast: Bacon-wrapped avocado bites

- Lunch: Keto Shrimp Salad

- Dinner: Keto Chicken Enchilada Bowl

Day 16

- Breakfast: Keto Cloud Eggs

- Lunch: Cauliflower Fried Rice

- Dinner: Buffalo Chicken Soup

Day 17

- Breakfast: Keto Zucchini Bread

- Lunch: Broccoli and Cheese Stuffed Bell Peppers

- Dinner: Walnut Crusted Salmon

Day 18

- Breakfast: Low Carb Bacon and Cheese Scones

- Lunch: Keto Spinach Salad with Feta and Walnuts

- Dinner: Keto Tuna Salad

Day 19

- Breakfast: Keto Burrito

- Lunch: Keto Arugula Salad with Halloumi and Balsamic Dressing

- Dinner: Cheese and Spinach Stuffed Chicken

Day 20

- Breakfast: Keto Sausage Breakfast Sandwich

- Lunch: Greek Chicken Salad

- Dinner: Salmon With Bacon & Tomato Cream Sauce

Day 21

- Breakfast: Popper Egg Cups

- Lunch: Keto Zucchini Salad with Ranch Dressing

- Dinner: Sheet Pan Chicken and Rainbow Veggies

Week 4

Day 22

- Breakfast: Keto Cinnamon Roll Knots

- Lunch: Keto Tuna Salad

- Dinner: Salmon & Asparagus Foil Packs

Day 23

- Breakfast: Keto Smoothie

- Lunch: Veggie Tacos

- Dinner: Creamy Tuscan Chicken

Day 24

- Breakfast: Avocado Toast with Eggs

- Lunch: Low Carb Mediterranean Quesadillas

- Dinner: Keto Salmon Cakes

Day 25

- Breakfast: Zucchini nacho chips

- Lunch: Guacamole with cucumber slices

- Dinner: Keto Eggplant Parmesan

Day 26

- Breakfast: Spinach Stuffed Mushroom

- Lunch: Crispy Tofu and Bok Choy Salad

- Dinner: Avocado & Basil Salmon

Day 27

- Breakfast: Bacon-wrapped avocado bites

- Lunch: Keto Shrimp Salad

- Dinner: Keto Chicken Enchilada Bowl

Day 28

- Breakfast: Keto Mug Cake

- Lunch: Keto Caesar Salad

- Dinner: Cheese and pepperoni chips (as a snack) + Keto Brownies

Remember to adjust portion sizes and ingredients to fit your individual dietary needs and preferences. Enjoy your delicious and varied 4-week keto meal plan!

Chapter 5

<u>Delicious Keto Breakfast Recipes</u>

<u>Keto biscuits and Gravy</u>

Ingredients

2 cups almond flour

1/4 cup coconut flour

2 tsp baking powder

1/2 tsp salt

1/3 cup margarine, liquefied

3/4 cup weighty cream

Instructions

1. Preheat your broiler to 350°F (175°C).

2. In a bowl, join almond flour, coconut flour, baking powder, and salt.

3. Mix in softened margarine and weighty cream until a batter structures.

4. Shape the mixture into rolls and put them on a baking sheet fixed with material paper.

5. Heat for 12-15 minutes or until the rolls are golden brown.

6. Present with your most loved keto-friendly sauce.

Details and Tips

Don't overmix the batter to guarantee delicate biscuit rolls.

Go ahead and add spices or ground cheddar for additional character.

For the sauce, use almond flour as a thickening specialist.

Cooking Times and Temperatures

Oven Preheat: 350°F (175°C)

Baking Time: 12-15 minutes

Visual Cues and Nutritional Info

The rolls ought to be golden brown when prepared.

Nutritional Info (per serving)

Calories: 220

Carbs: 5g

Protein: 6g

Fat: 20g

 Fiber: 3g

Net Carbs: 2g

Keto Sausage Breakfast Sandwich

Ingredients

2 huge eggs

2 sausage patties

2 cuts cheddar

Salt and pepper to taste

Spread for cooking

Instructions

1. Heat a skillet over medium intensity and liquefy a limited quantity of spread.

2. Cook the frankfurter patties until carmelized and cooked through. Put away.

3. In a bowl, whisk the eggs and season with salt and pepper.

4. Empty the whisked eggs into the skillet and cook, blending delicately, until they're mixed to your ideal consistency.

5. Put a cut of cheddar on top of each egg piece to dissolve.

6. Collect the sandwich by putting the fried eggs and sausage patty between two cheddar beat egg segments.

Details and Tips

Decide on wiener patties without added sugars.

Adjust with your cheddar and sauces.

Utilize a non-stick skillet to forestall staying.

Cooking Times and Temperatures

Cooking Time: According to bundle directions

Egg Scramble Time: 2-3 minutes

Visual Cues and Nutritional Info

Eggs ought to be completely cooked yet not overdone.

Nutritional Info (per serving)

Calories: 480

Carbs: 2g

Protein: 27g

Fat: 39g

Fiber: 0g

Net Carbs: 2g

Keto Cloud Eggs

Ingredients

2 big eggs

Salt and pepper to taste

Natural spices (discretionary)

Instructions

1. Preheat your oven to 350°F (175°C).

2. Separate egg whites and yolks cautiously, putting each in its own bowl.

3. Whip the egg whites until solid pinnacles structure. This might require a couple of moments.

4. Spoon the whipped egg whites onto a baking sheet fixed with material paper, making close to nothing "mists" with spaces in the middle.

5. Delicately slide one egg yolk into every space.

6. Heat in the preheated broiler for around 6-8 minutes, or until the egg whites are and the yolks are still marginally runny.

7. Season with salt, pepper, and new spices prior to serving.

Details and Tips

Utilize new eggs for simpler division.

Ensure there are no hints of egg yolk in the egg whites for fruitful whipping.

Experiment with various spices for added character.

Cooking Times and Temperatures

Broiler Preheat: 350°F (175°C)

Baking Time: 6-8 minutes

Visual Cues and Nutritional Info

 Egg whites ought to be golden and soft, yolks somewhat runny.

Nutritional Info (per serving)

 Calories: 160

 Carbs: 0g

 Protein: 14g

 Fat: 11g

 Fiber: 0g

 Net Carbs: 0g

 Keto Breakfast Casserole

Ingredients

- 6 eggs

- 1 cup prepared and disintegrated breakfast wiener

- 1 cup slashed spinach

- 1/2 cup destroyed cheddar

- 1/4 cup weighty cream

- Salt and pepper to taste

Instructions

1. Preheat your stove to 375°F (190°C).

2. In a bowl, whisk the eggs and weighty cream together. Season with salt and pepper.

3. Oil a baking dish and spread the cooked hotdog uniformly on the base.

4. Layer the slashed spinach on top of the hotdog.

5. Pour the egg blend over the wiener and spinach.

6. Sprinkle destroyed cheddar over the top.

7. Heat in the preheated stove for 20-25 minutes, or until the eggs are set and the cheddar is softened and effervescent.

8. Permit to cool somewhat prior to cutting and serving.

Details and Tips

customize with your vegetables and cheeses.

Guarantee the sausage is completely cooked prior to collecting the dish.

Cooking Times and Temperatures

Oven Preheat: 375°F (190°C)

Baking Time: 20-25 minutes

Visual Cues and Nutritional Info

The dish ought to be golden and firm.

Nutritional Info (per serving)

 - Calories: 320

 - Carbs: 2g

 - Protein: 19g

 - Fat: 26g

 - Fiber: 1g

 - Net Carbs: 1g

Keto Cinnamon Roll Knots

Ingredients

- 1 1/2 cups almond flour

- 2 tbsp coconut flour

- 2 tsp baking powder

- 1/4 cup erythritol (or favored keto-accommodating sugar)

- 1/2 tsp ground cinnamon

- Touch of salt

- 2 huge eggs

- 1/4 cup unsweetened almond milk

- 2 tbsp dissolved margarine

- 1 tsp vanilla concentrate

Instructions

1. Preheat your broiler to 350°F (175°C). Line a baking sheet with material paper.

2. In a bowl, whisk together almond flour, coconut flour, baking powder, erythritol, ground cinnamon, and salt.

3. In another bowl, beat the eggs, almond milk, softened spread, and vanilla concentrate.

4. Join the wet and dry ingredients to frame a mixture.

5. Partition the mixture into little parcels and roll each into a rope.

6. Structure each rope into a bunch shape and put on the pre-arranged baking sheet.

7. Prepare for 12-15 minutes, or until the bunches are brilliant and cooked through.

8. Permit to cool somewhat prior to serving.

Details and Tips

You can add a cream cheddar coat on top for added sweetness.

Adjust sweetness as you would prefer inclinations by adjusting how much sugar.

Cooking Times and Temperatures

Oven Preheat: 350°F (175°C)

Baking Time: 12-15 minutes

Visual Cues and Nutritional Info

Knots ought to be golden and firm to the touch.

Nutritional Info (per serving)

- Calories: 150

- Carbs: 5g

- Protein: 5g

- Fat: 13g

- Fiber: 3g

- Net Carbs: 2g

6. Keto Zucchini Bread

Ingredients

- 2 cups almond flour

- 1 tsp baking powder

- 1 tsp cinnamon

- 1/2 tsp salt

- 1 cup shredded zucchini

- 1/2 cup dissolved coconut oil

- 4 huge eggs

- 1/2 cup erythritol (or favored keto-accommodating sugar)

- 1 tsp vanilla concentrate

Step 1: Blend Dry Ingredients

- Preheat the oven to 350°F (175°C).

- In a bowl, consolidate almond flour, baking powder, cinnamon, and salt.

Step 2: Blend Wet Ingredients

- In a different bowl, blend destroyed zucchini, dissolved coconut oil, eggs, erythritol, and vanilla concentrate.

Step 3: mix and Bake

- Slowly add the wet blend into the dry combination and blend well.

- Empty the hitter into a lubed portion dish.

- Prepare for 50-60 minutes or until a toothpick tells the truth when embedded into the bread.

- Allow the bread to cool prior to cutting.

Details and Tips

Crush abundance dampness from the shredded zucchini prior to adding it to the blend.

Change sugar amount in view of your taste inclinations.

Store the bread in an impenetrable compartment in the cooler.

Cooking Time and Temperature

Prepare at 350°F (175°C) for 50-60 minutes.

Nutritional Info (per slice, approximate)

- Calories: 180

- Fat: 15g

- Protein: 6g

- Carbs: 6g

- Fiber: 2g

- Net Carbs: 4g

7. Low Carb Bacon and Cheese Scones

Ingredients

- 2 cups almond flour

- 1/4 cup coconut flour

- 1 tbsp baking powder

- 1/2 tsp salt

- 1/4 tsp dark pepper

- 1/3 cup cold spread, diced

- 1/2 cup cooked and disintegrated bacon

- 1 cup destroyed cheddar cheese

- 3 huge eggs

- 1/4 cup weighty cream

Step 1: Get ready Dough

Preheat the stove to 350°F (175°C).

In a bowl, join almond flour, coconut flour, baking powder, salt, and dark pepper.

Cut in the cold butter until the combination looks like coarse morsels.

Step 2: Add mix Ins

Blend in disintegrated bacon and destroyed cheddar cheese.

Step 3: Structure Scones

In a different bowl, whisk eggs and weighty cream.

Add the egg blend to the dry ingredients and blend until a mixture structures.

Partition the batter into equivalent parcels and shape them into scones.

Step 4: Bake

Put the scones on a baking sheet fixed with material paper.

Heat for 20-25 minutes or until the scones are golden brown.

Details and Tips

You can customize the add-ins with other keto-accommodating ingredients.

Ensure the spread is cold for flaky scones.

Allow the scones to cool somewhat prior to serving.

Cooking Time and Temperature

- Prepare at 350°F (175°C) for 20-25 minutes.

Nutritional Info (per scone, approximate)

- Calories: 230

- Fat: 20g

- Protein: 8g

- Carbs: 6g

- Fiber: 3g

- Net Carbs: 3g

<u>8. Keto Burrito</u>

Ingredients

- 2 enormous eggs

- 2 slices of bacon, cooked and disintegrated

- 1/4 avocado, sliced

- 2 tbsp destroyed cheddar cheese

- Salt and pepper to taste

Step 1: Get ready your Eggs ready

 Whisk the eggs in a bowl and season with salt and pepper.

 Cook the scrambled eggs in a non-stick skillet until done.

Step 2: Gather Burrito

Lay a huge lettuce leaf on a plate.

 Fill the leaf with fried eggs, bacon, avocado slices, and destroyed cheddar cheese.

Details and Tips

Utilize a solid lettuce leaf like chunk of ice or romaine to wrap the burrito.

Customize with your most loved keto-accommodating fillings.

Nutritional Info (per burrito, approximate)

- Calories: 350

- Fat: 29g

- Protein: 18g

- Carbs: 5g

- Fiber: 3g

- Net Carbs: 2g

9. Popper Egg Cups

Ingredients

- 6 huge eggs

- 1/4 cup diced chime peppers

- 1/4 cup diced jalapeños

- 1/2 cup destroyed cheddar cheese

- 1/4 cup cream cheese, mellowed

- Salt and pepper to taste

Step 1: Get ready Egg Mixture

Preheat the stove to 375°F (190°C).

In a bowl, beat the eggs and blend in diced peppers, jalapeños, destroyed cheddar cheese, and mellowed cream cheese.

Season with salt and pepper.

Step 2: Fill muffin Cups

- Grease a muffin tin or use silicone muffin cups.

- Empty the egg blend equally into the muffin cups.

Step 3: Bake

Prepare for 20-25 minutes or until the egg cups are set and somewhat brilliant on top.

Details and Tips

Change how much jalapeños in view of your zest inclination.

These egg cups are perfect for feast preparing.

Cooking Time and Temperature

Prepare at 375°F (190°C) for 20-25 minutes.

Nutritional Info (per egg cup, approximate)

- Calories: 100

- Fat: 8g

- Protein: 6g

- Carbs: 1.5g

- Fiber: 0.5g

- Net Carbs: 1g

10. Avocado Toast with Eggs

Ingredients

- 1 medium avocado, sliced

- 2 slices of keto bread (e.g., almond flour bread)

- 2 huge eggs

- Salt and pepper to taste

- Discretionary garnishes: red pepper chips, cleaved spices

Step 1: Toast Keto Bread

Toast the keto bread slices until they're fresh.

Step 2: Avocado

Pound or slice the avocado and spread it on the toasted bread slices.

Step 3: Cook Eggs

Cook the eggs (seared, poached, or bubbled) as indicated by your inclination.

Step 4: Gather Toast

Put the cooked eggs on top of the avocado-shrouded toast.

Season with salt and pepper, and add discretionary garnishes whenever wanted.

Details and Tips

Pick a great keto-accommodating bread or make your own.

Experiment with various egg arrangements for assortment.

Nutritional Info (per serving, approximate)

- Calories: 350

- Fat: 30g

- Protein: 12g

- Carbs: 9g

- Fiber: 7g

- Net Carbs: 2g

<u>11. Keto Waffles</u>

Ingredients

- 1 1/2 cups almond flour

- 2 tbsp coconut flour

- 1 tbsp baking powder

- 1/4 tsp salt

- 3 huge eggs

- 1/2 cup almond milk

- 2 tbsp dissolved margarine or coconut oil

- 1 tsp vanilla concentrate

- Discretionary: keto-accommodating sugar to taste

Step 1: Blend Dry Ingredients

Preheat the waffle iron.

In a bowl, whisk almond flour, coconut flour, baking powder, and salt.

Step 2: Prepare Batter

In a different bowl, whisk eggs, almond milk, liquefied spread or coconut oil, vanilla concentrate, and discretionary sugar.

Step 3: Join and Cook

Blend the wet ingredients into the dry ingredients until a player structures.

 Empty the player into the preheated waffle iron and cook until brilliant and firm.

Details and Tips

Cook waffles until they're very much sautéed for a superior surface.

The sugar is discretionary and can be changed in view of taste.

Cooking Time and Temperature

Follow your waffle iron's guidelines for cooking time.

Nutritional Info (per waffle, approximate)

- Calories: 250

- Fat: 20g

- Protein: 9g

- Carbs: 7g

- Fiber: 4g

- Net Carbs: 3g

12. Keto Smoothie

Ingredients

- 1/2 cup unsweetened almond milk

- 1/4 cup coconut milk

- 1/4 avocado

- 1/4 cup spinach

- 1/4 cup berries (e.g., raspberries, blueberries)

- 1 tbsp almond spread

- 1 scoop keto-accommodating protein powder (discretionary)

- Ice 3D shapes

Step 1: Mix Ingredients

Place all ingredients in a blender.

Step 2: Mix and Serve

Mix until smooth, changing almond milk or ice depending on the situation for wanted consistency.

Fill a glass and appreciate!

Details and Tips

Utilize a powerful blender for a smoother surface.

Go ahead and alter the ingredients and proportions as you would prefer.

Nutritional Info (entire smoothie, approximate)

- Calories: 300

- Fat: 25g

- Protein: 10g

- Carbs: 10g

- Fiber: 6g

- Net Carbs: 4g

Chapter 6

Keto Vegetarian Recipes

1. Spinach Stuffed Mushrooms

Ingredients

- large mushrooms

- Spinach

- Cream cheese

- Ground Parmesan

- Garlic

- Olive oil

- Salt and pepper

Step 1: Preheat the oven.

Step 2: Clean and eliminate comes from mushrooms.

Step 3: Sauté garlic, add spinach, and cook until withered.

Step 4: Blend spinach, cream cheese, Parmesan, salt, and pepper.

Step 5: Stuff mushrooms, top with Parmesan, and heat.

Details/Tips: Utilize enormous mushroom covers for simpler stuffing. Try not to overcook the spinach to hold tone.

Baking Time: 20 minutes

Temperature: 375°F (190°C)

Visual cue: Mushrooms are delicate and golden. Cheese is softened.

2. Zucchini Pasta with Creamy Avocado Pesto

Ingredients

- Zucchini

- Avocado

- Basil

- Lemon juice

- Garlic

- Pine nuts

- Olive oil

- Salt and pepper

Step 1: Spiralize zucchini into noodles.

Step 2: Mix avocado, basil, lemon juice, garlic, pine nuts.

Step 3: Add olive oil slowly to make pesto.

Step 4: Throw zucchini noodles in pesto.

Details/Tips: Add a touch of water in the event that pesto is excessively thick. Added lemon and garlic to taste.

Cooking Time: 15 minutes

Temperature: Room temperature

Visual cue: Zucchini noodles are covered equitably with pesto.

3. Keto Eggplant Parmesan

Ingredients

- Eggplant

- Almond flour

- Eggs

- Marinara sauce (without sugar)

- Mozzarella cheese

- Parmesan cheese

- Italian flavoring

Step 1: Cut eggplant, salt, and let sit to eliminate dampness.

Step 2: Dunk eggplant in egg, then, at that point, cover with almond flour.

Step 3: Broil covered eggplant until golden.

Step 4: Layer marinara, eggplant, mozzarella, and Parmesan.

Step 5: Heat until cheese is effervescent.

Details/Tips: Salting eggplant helps eliminate harshness and dampness.

Cooking Time: 30 minutes

Temperature: 375°F (190°C)

Visual cue: Cheese is softened and marginally sautéed.

4. Vegan Low Carb Keto Chili

Ingredients

- Cauliflower

- Bell peppers

- Onions

- Garlic

- Tomatoes

- Vegetable stock

- Chili powder

- Cumin

- Paprika

- black beans (discretionary)

- Avocado (for fixing)

Step 1: Sauté onions and garlic.

Step 2: Add bell peppers, cauliflower, tomatoes, stock, and flavors.

Step 3: Stew until veggies are delicate.

Step 4: Add dark beans whenever wanted.

Step 5: Serve finished off with avocado.

Details/Tips: You can substitute black beans with additional vegetables for lower carbs.

Cooking Time: 35 minutes

Temperature: Medium intensity

Visual cue: Vegetables are delicate, and flavors are very much joined.

5. Cauliflower Fried Rice

Ingredients

- Cauliflower

- Blended vegetables (peas, carrots, corn)

- Onions

- Garlic

- Soy sauce (or tamari for without gluten)

- Eggs

- Sesame oil

- Green onions

Step 1: pulse cauliflower in a food processor to rice-like texture.

Step 2: Sauté onions, garlic, and blended vegetables.

Step 3: Push veggies aside, scramble eggs.

Step 4: Add cauliflower, soy sauce, and sesame oil.

Step 5: Sautéed food until warmed, top with green onions.

Details/Tips: Guarantee veggies and cauliflower are cooked yet at the same time marginally crisp.

Cooking Time: 20 minutes

Temperature: Medium-high intensity

Visual cue: Cauliflower is delicate, and ingredients are all around blended.

6. Broccoli and Cheese Stuffed Bell Pepper

Ingredients

- Bell peppers

- Broccoli

- Cheddar cheese

- Cream cheese

- Garlic powder

- Onion powder

Step 1: Cut finishes off bell peppers, eliminate seeds.

Step 2: Steam broccoli until delicate fresh.

Step 3: Blend broccoli, cheddar, cream cheese, garlic, and onion powder.

Step 4: Stuff peppers with blend, heat until cheese is liquefied.

Details/Tips: Utilize an assortment of bell pepper combination for an engaging sight.

Cooking Time: 25 minutes

Temperature: 375°F (190°C)

Visual cue: Cheese is melted, and peppers are slightly softened.

7. Easy Keto Stuffed Eggplant

Ingredients

- Eggplant

- Olive oil

- Ricotta cheese

- Spinach

- Mozzarella cheese

- Marinara sauce (sans sugar)

Step 1: slice eggplant half, scoop out flesh.

Step 2: Brush with olive oil, heat until delicate.

Step 3: Blend ricotta, spinach, and mozzarella.

Step 4: Fill eggplant parts with combination, top with marinara.

Step 5: bake until cheese is bubbly.

Details/Tips: Pick more modest eggplants with less seeds.

Baking Time: 40 minutes

Temperature: 375°F (190°C)

Visual cue: Cheese is melted, and eggplant is softened.

8. Charred Veggie and Fried Goat Cheese Salad

Ingredients

- Leafy greens

- Zucchini

- Cherry tomatoes

- Red onion

- Goat cheese

- Olive oil

- Balsamic vinegar

Step 1: char zucchini and tomatoes on a grill or pan.

Step 2: Cut and sear goat cheese.

Step 3: Throw blended greens, charred veggies, and cheese.

Step 4: Shower with olive oil and balsamic vinegar.

Details/Tips: adjust grilling time for wanted char level.

Cooking Time: 15 minutes

Temperature: High intensity for grilling, medium-high for broiling

Visual cue: Veggies have grill marks, cheese is golden.

9. Keto Vegetarian Meatballs

Ingredients

- Pecans

- Eggs

- Parmesan cheese

- Garlic

- Onion

- Italian flavoring

- Marinara sauce (without sugar)

Step 1: pulse pecans, garlic, onion in a food processor.

Step 2: Add Parmesan, eggs, Italian flavoring, structure blend into balls.

Step 3: Prepare until brilliant.

Step 4: Warm marinara sauce, serve meatballs with sauce.

Details/Tips: Let the combination sit before to shaping to allow flavors to merge.

Baking Time: 25 minutes

Temperature: 375°F (190°C)

Visual cue: Meatballs are golden and firm.

10. Low Carb Mediterranean Quesadillas

Ingredients

- Low-carb tortillas

- Feta cheese

- Spinach

- Kalamata olives

- Sun-dried tomatoes

- Red onion

Step 1: Lay tortilla on a container, layer feta, spinach, olives, tomatoes, onion.

Step 2: Overlay tortilla, cook until cheese softens.

Step 3: Cut and present with tzatziki sauce.

Details/Tips: Be mindful so as not to overstuff to guarantee easy collapsing.

Cooking Time: 10 minutes

Temperature: Medium intensity

Visual Signal: Tortilla is fresh, cheese is melted.

11. Veggie Tacos

Ingredients

- Bell peppers

- Onions

- Mushrooms

- Zucchini

- Taco preparing

- Lettuce leaves (for wrapping)

- Avocado (for fixing)

Step 1: Sauté bell peppers, onions, mushrooms, zucchini.

Step 2: Add taco preparing, cook until veggies are delicate.

Step 3: Serve in lettuce leaves, top with avocado.

Details/Tips: Utilize various colourful veggies for a lively taco.

Cooking Time: 15 minutes

Temperature: Medium intensity

Visual Sign: Veggies are soft and prepared.

12. Crispy Tofu and Bok Choy Salad

Ingredients

- Tofu

- Bok choy

- Sesame oil

- Soy sauce

- Rice vinegar

- Ginger

- Sesame seeds

Step 1: Press and cube tofu, sauté until crispy.

Step 2: Sauté bok choy with sesame oil, soy sauce, ginger.

Step 3: Throw tofu and bok choy, sprinkle with rice vinegar.

Step 4: Sprinkle with sesame seeds.

Details/Tips: Utilize extra-firm tofu for better crisping.

Cooking Time: 20 minutes

Temperature: Medium-high intensity

Visual cue: Tofu is golden and fresh, bok choy is withered.

Chapter 7

Keto Salad Recipes

1. Greek Chicken Salad

Ingredients

1 pound boneless, skinless chicken bosoms, cooked and shredded

1/2 cup chopped cucumber

1/2 cup chopped tomato

1/4 cup chopped red onion

1/4 cup disintegrated feta cheddar

1/4 cup chopped new dill

1/4 cup olive oil

2 tablespoons red wine vinegar

1 teaspoon dried oregano

1/2 teaspoon salt

1/4 teaspoon dark pepper

Step

1. In an enormous bowl, mix the chicken, cucumber, tomato, red onion, feta cheddar, and dill.

2. In a little bowl, whisk together the olive oil, red wine vinegar, oregano, salt, and pepper.

3. Pour the dressing over the salad and prepare to cover.

Details and Tips

You can utilize any kind of lettuce you like for this salad.

In the event that you don't have new dill, you can substitute dried dill.

This salad can be made quite a bit early and put away in the fridge for as long as 3 days.

Cooking Times and Temperatures

None

Visual Cues

The chicken ought to be cooked through and shredded.

The vegetables ought to be chopped into scaled down pieces.

The salad ought to be equitably covered with the dressing.

Nutritional Info

Calories: 340

Fat: 24 grams

Protein: 28 grams

Starches: 5 grams

2. Keto Cajun Shrimp Caesar Salad

Ingredients

1 pound enormous shrimp, stripped and deveined

1 tablespoon olive oil

1 teaspoon Cajun preparing

1/2 cup shredded romaine lettuce

1/4 cup ground Parmesan cheddar

1/4 cup bread garnishes

1/4 cup Caesar dressing

Step

1. In an enormous skillet, heat the olive oil over medium intensity.

2. Add the shrimp and Cajun preparing and cook, blending sporadically, until the shrimp are pink and cooked through.

3. Remove the shrimp from the heat and set aside.

4. In a huge bowl, join the lettuce, Parmesan cheddar, bread garnishes, and Caesar dressing.

5. Add the shrimp and toss to coat.

Details and Tips

You can utilize any sort of lettuce you like for this salad.

On the off chance that you don't have Cajun preparing, you can substitute a blend of paprika, cayenne pepper, garlic powder, onion powder, and salt.

This salad can be made early and put away in the cooler for as long as 3 days.

Cooking Times and Temperatures

Shrimp: 3-5 minutes

Temperature: none

Visual Cues

The shrimp ought to be pink and cooked through.

The salad ought to be equally covered with the dressing.

Nutritional Info

Calories: 370

Fat: 26 grams

Protein: 28 grams

Carbohydrates: 5 grams

3. Keto Cobb Salad

Ingredients

1/2 cup shredded cooked chicken wings

1/2 cup shredded cooked bacon

1/4 cup disintegrated blue cheddar

1/4 cup chopped hard-bubbled egg

1/4 cup chopped tomato

1/4 cup chopped avocado

1/4 cup shredded lettuce

2 tablespoons ranch dressing

Step

1. In an enormous bowl, join the chicken, bacon, blue cheddar, hard-bubbled egg, tomato, avocado, and lettuce.

2. Sprinkle with the ranch dressing and throw to cover.

Details and Tips

You can utilize any kind of lettuce you like for this salad.

You can likewise add different ingredients to this salad, like shredded cheddar, bread garnishes, or nuts.

This salad can be made somewhat early and put away in the fridge for as long as 3 days.

Cooking Times and Temperatures

None

Visual Cues

The chicken, bacon, and egg ought to be cooked through.

The avocado ought to be ready.

4. Keto Tuna Salad

Ingredients

1 can (12 ounces) tuna, depleted and chipped

1/2 cup mayonnaise

1/4 cup celery, chopped

1/4 cup onion, chopped

1/4 teaspoon salt

1/8 teaspoon black pepper

Step

1. In a medium bowl, join the tuna, mayonnaise, celery, onion, salt, and pepper.

2. Mix until very much consolidated.

Details and Tips

You can utilize any kind of mayonnaise you like for this salad.

You can likewise add different ingredients to this salad, like chopped pickles, mustard, or dill.

This salad can be made somewhat early and put away in the fridge for as long as 3 days.

Cooking Times and Temperatures

None

Visual Cues

The tuna ought to be chipped.

The vegetables ought to be chopped into reduced down pieces.

The salad ought to be equitably covered with the mayonnaise.

Nutritional Info

Calories: 230

Fat: 20 grams

Protein: 20 grams

Sugars: 2 grams

5. Keto Egg Salad

Ingredients

6 hard-bubbled eggs, stripped and chopped

1/2 cup mayonnaise

1/4 cup celery, chopped

1/4 teaspoon salt

1/8 teaspoon dark pepper

Step

1. In a medium bowl, join the eggs, mayonnaise, celery, salt, and pepper.

2. Mix until very much joined.

Details and Tips

You can utilize any kind of mayonnaise you like for this salad.

You can likewise add different ingredients to this salad, like chopped mustard, dill, or paprika.

This salad can be made early and put away in the fridge for as long as 3 days.

Cooking Times and Temperatures

Eggs: 10-12 minutes

Visual Cues

The eggs ought to be hard-bubbled and chopped.

The vegetables ought to be chopped into reduced down pieces.

The salad ought to be equitably covered with the mayonnaise.

Nutritional Info

Calories: 260

Fat: 20 grams

Protein: 18 grams

Sugars: 2 grams

6. Antipasto Salad

Ingredients

1/2 cup shredded mozzarella cheddar

1/4 cup chopped salami

1/4 cup chopped pepperoni

1/4 cup chopped artichoke hearts

1/4 cup chopped dark olives

1/4 cup chopped tomatoes

1/4 cup shredded lettuce

2 tablespoons Italian dressing

Step

1. In an enormous bowl, join the mozzarella cheddar, salami, pepperoni, artichoke hearts, dark olives, tomatoes, and lettuce.

2. Sprinkle with the Italian dressing and throw to cover.

Details and Tips

 You can utilize any kind of lettuce you like for this salad.

You can likewise add different ingredients to this salad, like chopped ham, cheddar, or nuts.

 This salad can be made quite a bit early and kept in the cooler for as long as 3 days.

Cooking Times and Temperatures

None

Visual Cues

The cheddar ought to be shredded.

The meats ought to be chopped.

The vegetables ought to be chopped into reduced smallest pieces.

The salad ought to be equally covered with the dressing.

Nutritional Info

Calories: 400

Fat: 30 grams

Protein: 20 grams

Sugars: 5 grams

7. Keto Spinach Salad with Feta and Walnuts

Ingredients

1/2 cup disintegrated feta cheddar

1/4 cup chopped walnuts

1/4 cup olive oil

2 tablespoons lemon juice

1 teaspoon dried oregano

1/2 teaspoon salt

1/4 teaspoon dark pepper

1/2 cup spinach leaves

Step

1. In a little bowl, consolidate the feta cheddar, walnuts, olive oil, lemon juice, oregano, salt, and pepper.

2. Turn continuously until very much joined.

3. Add the spinach leaves and toss to coat.

Details and Tips

You can likewise add different ingredients to this salad, like chopped strawberries, cucumbers, or tomatoes.

This salad can be made early and put away in the fridge for as long as 3 days.

Cooking Times and Temperatures

None

Visual Cues

The feta cheddar ought to be disintegrated.

The walnuts ought to be chopped.

The spinach leaves ought to be washed and dried.

The salad ought to be equitably covered with the dressing.

Nutritional Info

Calories: 250

 Fat: 20 grams

 Protein: 10 grams

 Carbs: 5 grams

8. Keto Arugula Salad with Halloumi and Balsamic Dressing

Ingredients

1/2 cup disintegrated halloumi cheddar

1/4 cup balsamic vinegar

2 tablespoons olive oil

1 teaspoon Dijon mustard

1/2 teaspoon salt

1/4 teaspoon dark pepper

 1 cup arugula leaves

Step

1. In a little bowl, whisk together the balsamic vinegar, olive oil, Dijon mustard, salt, and pepper.

2. Add the arugula leaves and throw to cover.

3. Top with the halloumi cheddar and serve.

Details and Tips

You can likewise add different ingredients to this salad, like chopped tomatoes, cucumbers, or nuts.

This salad can be made quite a bit early and stored in the cooler for as long as 3 days.

Cooking Times and Temperatures

Halloumi cheddar: 2-3 minutes for each side

Visual Cues

The halloumi cheddar ought to be golden brown and firm.

The arugula leaves ought to be washed and dried.

The salad ought to be equitably covered with the dressing.

Nutritional Info

Calories: 300

Fat: 25 grams

Protein: 15 grams

Sugars: 5 grams

9. Keto Zucchini Salad with Ranch Dressing

Ingredients

1 medium zucchini, shredded

1/2 cup chopped onion

1/4 cup chopped celery

1/4 cup ranch dressing

1/4 teaspoon salt

1/8 teaspoon dark pepper

Step

1. In an enormous bowl, join the zucchini, onion, celery, ranch dressing, salt, and pepper.

2. Toss to coat.

Details and Tips

You can likewise add different ingredients to this salad, like chopped

tomatoes, cucumbers, or nuts.

This salad can be made quite a bit early and put away in the fridge for as long as 3 days.

Cooking Times and Temperatures

None

Visual Cues

The zucchini ought to be shredded.

The vegetables ought to be chopped into scaled down pieces.

The salad ought to be uniformly covered with the dressing.

Nutritional Info

Calories: 150

Fat: 10 grams

Protein: 5 grams

Sugars: 5 grams

10. Keto Salmon Salad

Ingredients

1 (4 ounce) salmon filet, cooked and chipped

1/2 cup chopped cucumber

1/4 cup chopped red onion

1/4 cup chopped dill

1/4 cup olive oil

2 tablespoons lemon juice

1 teaspoon Dijon mustard

1/2 teaspoon salt

1/4 teaspoon dark pepper

Step

1. In an enormous bowl, join the salmon, cucumber, red onion, dill, olive oil, lemon juice, Dijon mustard, salt, and pepper.

2. Mix until all around joined.

3. Serve on lettuce leaves or wafers.

11. Keto Shrimp Salad

Ingredients

1 pound cooked shrimp, stripped and deveined

1/2 cup slashed celery

1/4 cup slashed red onion

1/4 cup mayonnaise

2 tablespoons lemon juice

1 teaspoon Dijon mustard

1/2 teaspoon salt

1/4 teaspoon dark pepper

Step

1. In an enormous bowl, consolidate the shrimp, celery, red onion, mayonnaise, lemon juice, Dijon mustard, salt, and pepper.

2. Mix until all around joined.

3. Serve on lettuce leaves or wafers.

Details and Tips

You can likewise add different ingredients to this salad, like slashed avocado, tomatoes, or nuts.

This salad can be made somewhat early and put away in the cooler for as long as 3 days.

Cooking Times and Temperatures

Shrimp: 3-5 minutes

Visual Cues

The shrimp ought to be cooked through and stripped.

The vegetables ought to be slashed into scaled down pieces.

The salad ought to be equally covered with the dressing.

Nutritional Info

Calories: 300

Fat: 20 grams

Protein: 30 grams

Sugars: 5 grams

12. Keto Caesar Salad

Ingredients

1 head romaine lettuce, slashed

1/2 cup bread garnishes

1/4 cup ground Parmesan cheddar

2 tablespoons Caesar dressing

Step

1. In an enormous bowl, consolidate the lettuce, bread garnishes, Parmesan cheddar, and Caesar dressing.

2. Toss to coat.

Details and Tips

You can likewise add different ingredients to this salad, like cooked chicken, shrimp, or bacon.

This salad can be made early and put away in the cooler for as long as 3 days.

Cooking Times and Temperatures

None

Visual Cues

The lettuce ought to be chopped into scaled down pieces.

The bread garnishes ought to be uniformly disseminated all through the salad.

The salad ought to be equitably covered with the dressing.

Nutritional Info

Calories: 200

Fat: 15 grams

Protein: 10 grams

Carbohydrates: 5 grams

Chapter 8

Tasty keto Snacks and Appetizers

1. Bacon-wrapped avocado bites

Ingredients

2 avocados, split and pitted

12 slices of bacon

1/4 teaspoon garlic powder

1/4 teaspoon onion powder

Salt and pepper to taste

Steps

1. Preheat broiler to 400 degrees F (200 degrees C).

2. Wrap every avocado half with 2 slices of bacon.

3. Sprinkle with garlic powder, onion powder, salt, and pepper.

4. Prepare in preheated broiler for 20-25 minutes, or until bacon is cooked through.

Details and Tips

You can utilize any kind of bacon you like.

If you have any desire to make these quite a bit early, you can enclose the avocado parts by bacon and then, at that point, freeze them. At the point when you're prepared to heat them, defrost them short-term in the fridge and then, at that point, heat as coordinated.

These avocado bites are likewise tasty presented with a dipping sauce, for example, farm dressing or guacamole.

Cooking Times and Temperatures

Preheat broiler to 400 degrees F (200 degrees C).

Heat in preheated stove for 20-25 minutes, or until bacon is cooked through.

Visual cue

The bacon ought to be cooked through and the avocado ought to be delicate.

Nutritional Info

Calories: 200

Fat: 18g

Protein: 6g

Carbs: 3g

2. Zucchini nacho chips

Ingredients

2 medium zucchini, cut into 1/4-inch thick adjusts

1 tablespoon olive oil

1/2 teaspoon salt

1/4 teaspoon dark pepper

Steps

1. Preheat broiler to 400 degrees F (200 degrees C).

2. Brush zucchini slices with olive oil.

3. Sprinkle with salt and pepper.

4. Prepare in preheated stove for 10-15 minutes, or until brilliant brown and fresh.

Details and Tips

You can utilize any sort of zucchini you like.

If you have any desire to make these somewhat early, you can cut the zucchini and then, at that point, store it in the cooler for as long as 24 hours. At the point when you're prepared to heat them, just brush them with olive oil and heat as coordinated.

These zucchini nacho chips are likewise tasty presented with various garnishes, like guacamole, salsa, and cheese.

Cooking Times and Temperatures

Preheat stove to 400 degrees F (200 degrees C).

Prepare in preheated stove for 10-15 minutes, or until golden brown and firm.

Visual cue

The zucchini slices ought to be brown and fresh.

Nutritional Info

Calories: 100

Fat: 8g

Protein: 2g

Carbs: 4g

3. Cheese and pepperoni chips

Ingredients

12 slices of cheese

12 slices of pepperoni

Steps

1. Preheat broiler to 350 degrees F (175 degrees C).

2. Put a cut of cheese on top of a cut of pepperoni.

3. Rehash until the cheese and pepperoni slices are all utilized.

4. Prepare in preheated stove for 5-7 minutes, or until cheese is dissolved and effervescent.

Details and Tips

You can utilize any kind of cheese you like.

To make these somewhat early, you can gather the chips and then freeze them. At the point when you're prepared to heat them, defrost them short-term in the fridge and then prepare as coordinated.

These cheese and pepperoni chips are likewise heavenly presented with a dipping sauce, for example, marinara sauce or farm dressing.

Cooking Times and Temperatures

Preheat broiler to 350 degrees F (175 degrees C).

Heat in preheated stove for 5-7 minutes, or until cheese is dissolved and effervescent.

Visual cue

The cheese ought to be softened and effervescent.

Nutritional Info

Calories: 100

Fat: 8g

Protein: 3g

Carbs: 1g

4. Guacamole with cucumber

Ingredients

2 avocados, crushed

1/2 cucumber, diced

1/4 onion, diced

1/4 cup cilantro, hacked

1 tablespoon lime juice

1/2 teaspoon salt

1/4 teaspoon dark pepper

Steps

1. In a bowl, consolidate the ingredients as a whole.

2. Mix well.

3. Present with tortilla chips, cucumber slices, or celery sticks.

Details and Tips

You can utilize any kind of cucumber you like.

 To make this quite a bit early, you can store it in the fridge for as long as 24 hours.

This guacamole is likewise tasty presented with various different garnishes, like tomatoes, jalapeños, or bacon bits.

Cooking Times and Temperatures

 None

Visual cue

The guacamole ought to be a creamy green tone.

Nutritional Info

Calories: 150

Fat: 13g

Protein: 2g

Carbs: 7g

5. Deviled eggs with bacon

Ingredients

6 hard-boiled eggs, stripped and split

2 tablespoons mayonnaise

1 tablespoon Dijon mustard

1 teaspoon apple juice vinegar

1/2 teaspoon salt

1/4 teaspoon dark pepper

4 slices bacon, cooked and disintegrated

Steps

1. In a bowl, consolidate the mayonnaise, mustard, vinegar, salt, and pepper.

2. Squash the egg yolks into the mayonnaise mixture.

3. Spoon the egg yolk mixture into the egg whites.

4. Top with disintegrated bacon.

Details and Tips

You can utilize any kind of mayonnaise you like.

To make these somewhat early, you can collect the deviled eggs and then store them in the fridge for as long as 24 hours.

These deviled eggs are likewise delectable presented with various different fixings, like paprika, chives, or parsley.

Cooking Times and Temperatures

Hard-heat up the eggs for 10-12 minutes.

Visual cue

The egg yolks ought to be mashed and smooth.

Nutritional Info:

Calories: 150

Fat: 12g

Protein: 7g

Carbs: 1g

6. Buffalo cauliflower bites

Ingredients:

1 head cauliflower, cut into florets

1/2 cup hot sauce

1/4 cup margarine, dissolved

1/4 cup garlic powder

1/4 teaspoon salt

1/4 teaspoon dark pepper

Steps

1. Preheat broiler to 400 degrees F (200 degrees C).

2. In an enormous bowl, join the cauliflower, hot sauce, margarine, garlic powder, salt, and pepper.

3. Toss to coat.

4. Spread the cauliflower florets in a solitary layer on a baking sheet.

5. Heat in preheated broiler for 20-25 minutes, or until brilliant brown and delicate.

Details and Tips

You can utilize any kind of hot sauce you like.

If you have any desire to make these somewhat early, you can collect the cauliflower florets and then, at that point, store them in the fridge for as long as 24 hours. At the point when you're prepared to heat them, just heat

as coordinated.

These buffalo cauliflower bites are likewise scrumptious presented with an assortment of dipping sauces, for example, farm dressing or blue cheese dressing.

Cooking Times and Temperatures:

Preheat oven to 400 degrees F (200 degrees C).

Prepare in preheated broiler for 20-25 minutes, or until brilliant brown and delicate.

Visual cue

The cauliflower florets ought to be golden brown and delicate.

Nutritional Info

Calories: 150

Fat: 12g

Protein: 4g

Carbs: 5g

7. Mini cheeseburger sliders (lettuce wrapped)

Ingredients

1 pound ground meat

1/2 onion, diced

1/2 teaspoon salt

1/4 teaspoon dark pepper

12 burger buns, lettuce-wrapped

1/2 cup destroyed cheddar cheese

1/4 cup ketchup

1/4 cup mustard

 Lettuce leaves, for serving

Steps

1. Preheat stove to 350 degrees F (175 degrees C).

2. In a huge bowl, join the ground meat, onion, salt, and pepper.

3. Mix well.

4. Structure the ground meat mixture into 12 little patties.

5. Put the patties on a baking sheet.

6. Heat in preheated stove for 10-12 minutes, or until cooked through.

7. Top every patty with cheese, ketchup, and mustard.

8. Serve on lettuce-wrapped burger buns.

Details and Tips

You can utilize any sort of cheese you like.

To make these somewhat early, you can collect the sliders and then, at that point, prepare them as coordinated prior to serving.

These mini cheeseburger sliders are likewise heavenly presented with different fixings, like pickles, onions, or bacon.

Cooking Times and Temperatures:

Preheat broiler to 350 degrees F (175 degrees C).

Heat in preheated oven for 10-12 minutes, or until cooked through.

Visual cue

The patties ought to be cooked through and the cheese ought to be dissolved.

Nutritional Info

Calories: 200

Fat: 16g

Protein: 10g

Carbs: 4g

8. Spinach and artichoke dip with veggie sticks

Ingredients

1 (10 ounce) bundle frozen cleaved spinach, defrosted and depleted

1 (14 ounce) can artichoke hearts, depleted and cleaved

1/2 cup mayonnaise

1/4 cup ground Parmesan cheese

1/4 teaspoon garlic powder

1/4 teaspoon salt

1/8 teaspoon dark pepper

Veggie sticks, for serving

Steps

1. In a medium bowl, consolidate the spinach, artichoke hearts, mayonnaise, Parmesan cheese, garlic powder, salt, and pepper.

2. Mix well.

3. Present with veggie sticks.

Details and Tips

You can utilize any kind of veggie sticks you like.

To make this early, you can collect the dip and then store it in the fridge for as long as 24 hours.

This spinach and artichoke dip is additionally tasty presented with wafers or pita bread.

Cooking Times and Temperatures

None

Visual cue

 The dip ought to be creamy and smooth.

Nutritional Info

Calories: 150

 Fat: 12g

Protein: 3g

Carbs: 5g

9. Keto-friendly trail mix (nuts and seeds)

Ingredients

1 cup almonds

1/2 cup walnuts

1/4 cup walnuts

1/4 cup sunflower seeds

1/4 cup pumpkin seeds

1/4 cup chia seeds

1/4 teaspoon salt

Steps

1. In a huge bowl, consolidate the ingredients in general.

2. Mix well.

3. Store in a air tight holder at room temperature.

Details and Tips

You can utilize any kind of nuts and seeds you like.

This keto-friendly trail mix is likewise scrumptious presented with yogurt or natural product.

Cooking Times and Temperatures

None

Visual cue

The nuts and seeds ought to be uniformly mixed.

Nutritional Info

Calories: 200

Fat: 18g

Protein: 5g

Carbs: 5g

10. Smoked salmon and cream cheese roll-ups

Ingredients

1 (8 ounce) bundle smoked salmon, daintily cut

1 (8 ounce) bundle cream cheese, mellowed

1/4 cup hacked chives

1/4 teaspoon salt

1/8 teaspoon dark pepper

Lettuce leaves, for serving

Steps

1. In a little bowl, consolidate the cream cheese, chives, salt, and pepper.

2. Mix well.

3. Spread the cream cheese mixture on the smoked salmon slices.

4. Roll up the smoked salmon slices

4. Roll up the smoked salmon slices and secure with a toothpick.

5. Serve on lettuce leaves.

Details and Tips

You can utilize any kind of chives you like.

If you have any desire to make these early, you can gather the roll-ups and then store them in the cooler for as long as 24 hours.

These smoked salmon and cream cheese roll-ups are likewise flavorful presented with various different garnishes, like tricks, dill, or lemon juice.

Cooking Times and Temperatures

None

Visual cue

The roll-ups ought to be flawlessly rolled and secure.

Nutritional Info

Calories: 150

Fat: 12g

Protein: 10g

Carbs: 2g

11. Parmesan zucchini fries

Ingredients

2 medium zucchini, cut into 1/4-inch thick adjusts

1/2 cup ground Parmesan cheese

1/4 teaspoon garlic powder

1/4 teaspoon salt

1/8 teaspoon dark pepper

Olive oil, for broiling

Steps

1. Preheat oven to 400 degrees F (200 degrees C).

2. In a medium bowl, consolidate the Parmesan cheese, garlic powder, salt, and pepper.

3. Dip the zucchini slices in the Parmesan mixture.

4. Put the zucchini slices on a baking sheet.

5. Shower with olive oil.

6. Prepare in preheated oven for 10-15 minutes, or until brilliant brown and fresh.

Details and Tips

You can utilize any sort of zucchini you like.

If you have any desire to make these early, you can cut the zucchini and then, at that point, store it in the cooler for as long as 24 hours. At the point when you're prepared to heat them, basically dip them in the Parmesan mixture and heat as coordinated.

These Parmesan zucchini fries are likewise tasty presented with an assortment of dipping sauces, for example, marinara sauce or farm dressing.

Cooking Times and Temperatures

Preheat oven to 400 degrees F (200 degrees C).

Heat in preheated oven for 10-15 minutes, or until brilliant brown and firm.

Visual cue

The zucchini slices ought to be golden brown and firm.

Nutritional Info:

Calories: 100

Fat: 8g

Protein: 3g

Carbs: 4g

12. Bacon-wrapped jalapeno poppers

Ingredients

12 jalapeno peppers, divided and cultivated

1/2 cup cream cheese, relaxed

1/4 cup destroyed cheddar cheese

1/4 teaspoon garlic powder

1/4 teaspoon salt

1/8 teaspoon dark pepper

12 slices of bacon

Steps

1. Preheat oven to 400 degrees F (200 degrees C).

2. In a little bowl, join the cream cheese, cheddar cheese, garlic powder, salt, and pepper.

3. Mix well.

4. Stuff the cream cheese mixture into the jalapeno parts.

5. Wrap every jalapeno half with a cut of bacon.

6. Put the jalapeno poppers on a baking sheet.

7. Bake in preheated oven for 15-20 minutes, or until the bacon is cooked

through.

Details and Tips

You can utilize any kind of cream cheese you like.

If you have any desire to make these early, you can collect the poppers and then prepare them as coordinated prior to serving.

These bacon-wrapped jalapeno poppers are likewise delectable presented with an assortment of dipping sauces, for example, farm dressing or blue cheese dressing.

Cooking Times and Temperatures:

Preheat oven to 400 degrees F (200 degrees C).

Bake in preheated oven for 15-20 minutes, or until the bacon is cooked through.

Visual cue

The bacon ought to be cooked through and the jalapenos ought to be delicate.

Nutritional Info

Calories: 200

Fat: 16g

Protein: 9g

Carbs: 3g

Chapter 9

Decadent Keto Desserts

1. Keto Mug Cake

Ingredients

1/4 cup almond flour

1/4 teaspoon baking powder

1/4 teaspoon baking pop

1/4 teaspoon salt

1 tablespoon granulated sugar

1 tablespoon margarine, liquefied

1 egg

1 tablespoon weighty cream

1/2 teaspoon vanilla concentrate

Steps

1. In a mug, whisk together the almond flour, baking powder, baking pop, and salt.

2. Mix in the sugar, margarine, egg, cream, and vanilla concentrate until recently consolidated.

3. Microwave on high for 1-2 minutes, or until the cake is set.

Details and tips

For a more extravagant flavor, utilize dim chocolate almond flour.

 In the event that you don't have a microwave, you can prepare the mug cake in a preheated broiler at 350 degrees Fahrenheit for 15-20 minutes, or until the cake is set.

Top the mug cake with your most loved keto-accommodating garnishes, like whipped cream, berries, or chocolate sauce.

Cooking time and temperature

Microwave: 1-2 minutes

Oven : 350 degrees Fahrenheit, 15-20 minutes

Visual cues

The cake will be set and brilliant brown on top.

Nutritional info (per serving)

Calories: 150

 Fat: 12 grams

Protein: 5 grams

Net carbs: 3 grams

2. Keto Chocolate Lava Cakes

Ingredients

1/4 cup almond flour

1/4 teaspoon baking powder

1/4 teaspoon baking pop

1/4 teaspoon salt

1 tablespoon granulated sugar

1 tablespoon margarine, dissolved

1 egg

1 tablespoon weighty cream

1/2 teaspoon vanilla concentrate

1 tablespoon sans sugar chocolate chips

Steps

1. Preheat oven to 350 degrees Fahrenheit.

2. Oil four ramekins with margarine or cooking splash.

3. In a bowl, whisk together the almond flour, baking powder, baking pop,

and salt.

4. Mix in the sugar, margarine, egg, cream, and vanilla concentrate until recently consolidated.

5. Overlap in the chocolate chips.

6. Partition the player uniformly among the pre-arranged ramekins.

7. Heat for 10-12 minutes, or until the cakes are set and the chocolate is softened.

Details and tips

For a more extravagant flavor, utilize dull chocolate almond flour.

Allow the cakes to cool for a couple of moments prior to serving.

Serve the cakes quickly with your most loved keto-accommodating garnishes, like whipped cream, berries, or chocolate sauce.

Cooking time and temperature

Oven : 350 degrees Fahrenheit, 10-12 minutes

Visual cues

The cakes will be set and the chocolate will be melted.

Nutritional info (per serving)

Calories: 180

Fat: 15 grams

Protein: 5 grams

Net carbs: 3 grams

3. Keto Cheesecake

Ingredients

1 cup almond flour

1/4 cup granulated sugar

1/4 teaspoon baking powder

1/4 teaspoon salt

1/2 cup margarine, mellowed

3 eggs

1 cup weighty cream

1 teaspoon vanilla concentrate

1/2 cup sans sugar chocolate chips

Steps

1. Preheat broiler to 350 degrees Fahrenheit.

2. Oil a 9-inch springform container with spread or cooking shower.

3. In a bowl, whisk together the almond flour, sugar, baking powder, and

salt.

4. In a different bowl, beat together the margarine and eggs until light and cushioned.

5. Beat in the weighty cream and vanilla concentrate until consolidated.

6. Crease the dry ingredients into the wet ingredients until recently joined.

7. Mix in the chocolate chips.

8. Empty the hitter into the pre-arranged skillet and heat for 30-35 minutes, or until the cheesecake is set.

Details and tips

For a more extravagant flavor, utilize dull chocolate almond flour.

Allow the cheesecake to cool totally prior to serving.

Top the cheesecake with your most loved keto-accommodating fixings, like whipped cream, berries, or chocolate sauce.

You can likewise make a keto cheesecake outside by combining as one 1 cup of almond flour, 1/4 cup of margarine, and 1/4 cup of granulated sugar. Press the hull into the lower part of the springform skillet prior to adding the cheesecake player.

To make a keto cheesecake filling, you can utilize 1 cup of cream cheddar, 1/2 cup of sharp cream, 1/4 cup of granulated sugar, 3 eggs, and 1 teaspoon of vanilla concentrate. Beat the ingredients together until smooth.

You can likewise add different flavors to the cheesecake, like lemon, raspberry, or chocolate.

Cooking time and temperature

Oven: 350 degrees Fahrenheit, 30-35 minutes

Visual cues

The cheesecake will be set and the top will be golden brown.

Nutritional info (per serving)

Calories: 300

Fat: 25 grams

Protein: 10 grams

Net carbs: 5 grams

4. Keto Brownies

Ingredients

1 cup almond flour

1/4 cup unsweetened cocoa powder

1/4 cup granulated sugar

1/4 teaspoon baking powder

1/4 teaspoon salt

1/4 cup margarine, dissolved

2 eggs

1 tablespoon weighty cream

1 teaspoon vanilla concentrate

Steps

1. Preheat oven to 350 degrees Fahrenheit.

2. Oil a 8x8 inch baking skillet with spread or cooking splash.

3. In a bowl, whisk together the almond flour, cocoa powder, sugar, baking powder, and salt.

4. Mix in the margarine, eggs, cream, and vanilla concentrate until recently consolidated.

5. Empty the hitter into the pre-arranged skillet and heat for 25-30 minutes, or until a toothpick embedded into the middle confesses all.

Details and tips

For a more extravagant flavor, utilize dull cocoa powder.

Allow the brownies to cool totally prior to cutting and serving.

Top the brownies with your most loved keto-accommodating garnishes, like whipped cream, chocolate sauce, or nuts.

Cooking time and temperature

Oven: 350 degrees Fahrenheit, 25-30 minutes

Visual cues

The brownies will be set and the top will be slightly cracked.

Nutritional info (per serving)

Calories: 200

Fat: 15 grams

Protein: 5 grams

*Net carbs: 5 grams

5. Keto Cookies

Ingredients

1 cup almond flour

1/4 cup granulated sugar

1/4 teaspoon baking powder

1/4 teaspoon salt

1/4 cup margarine, mellowed

1 egg

* 1 teaspoon vanilla concentrate

Steps:

1. Preheat broiler to 350 degrees Fahrenheit.

2. Line a baking sheet with material paper.

3. In a bowl, whisk together the almond flour, sugar, baking powder, and salt.

4. Mix in the spread, egg, and vanilla concentrate until recently consolidated.

5. Drop the batter by adjusted tablespoons onto the pre-arranged baking sheet.

6. Prepare for 10-12 minutes, or until the cookies are set.

Details and tips

 For a chewier treat, cool the batter for 30 minutes prior to baking.

Allow the cookies to cool totally before putting them in an impenetrable compartment.

Top the cookies with your most loved keto-accommodating fixings, like chocolate chips, nuts, or sans sugar sprinkles.

Cooking time and temperature

Oven: 350 degrees Fahrenheit, 10-12 minutes

Visual cues

The cookies will be set and golden brown on the base.

Nutritional info (per treat)

 Calories: 100

Fat: 9 grams

Protein: 2 grams

 Net carbs: 2 grams

6. Keto Ice Cream

Ingredients

1 cup weighty cream

 1/2 cup almond milk

 1/4 cup granulated sugar

1/4 teaspoon vanilla concentrate

1/4 teaspoon thickener

 1/4 cup without sugar chocolate chips (discretionary)

Steps

1. In a blender, consolidate the weighty cream, almond milk, sugar, vanilla concentrate, and thickener. Mix until smooth.

2. Empty the blend into an ice cream creator and stir as per the producer's guidelines.

3. Mix in the chocolate chips, if utilizing.

4. Move the ice cream to a cooler safe compartment and freeze for no less than 4 hours prior to serving.

Details and tips:

You can likewise utilize coconut milk rather than almond milk.

 To make a keto ice cream base, you can join 1 cup of weighty cream, 1/2 cup of almond milk, and 1/4 cup of granulated sugar in a pan. Heat over medium intensity until the sugar is broken up.

 To make keto ice cream sandwiches, spread the ice cream between two keto-accommodating cookies.

Cooking time and temperature

No cooking required

Visual cues

The ice cream will be smooth and creamy.

Nutritional info (per serving)

Calories: 200

Fat: 15 grams

Protein: 5 grams

Net carbs: 5 grams

7. Keto Fat Bombs

Ingredients

1/2 cup almond margarine

1/4 cup coconut oil, liquefied

1/4 cup granulated sugar

1/4 teaspoon vanilla concentrate

1/4 cup sans sugar chocolate chips (discretionary)

Steps

1. In a bowl, join the almond spread, coconut oil, sugar, and vanilla concentrate. Blend until smooth.

2. Mix in the chocolate chips, if utilizing.

3. Shape the combination into balls and put them on a material lined

baking sheet.

4. Freeze for no less than 2 hours prior to serving.

Details and tips

You can likewise utilize other keto-accommodating ingredients in your fat bombs, for example, cocoa powder, nuts, or seeds.

To make various fat bombs, attempt various kinds of sugar and chocolate chips.

Cooking time and temperature:

No cooking required

Visual cues

The fat bombs will be firm and round.

Nutritional info (per fat bomb)

Calories: 100

Fat: 10 grams

Protein: 1 gram

Net carbs: 1 gram

Ingredients

1 cup almond flour

1/4 cup granulated sugar

1/4 teaspoon baking powder

1/4 teaspoon salt

1/4 cup margarine, liquefied

1 egg

1 tablespoon weighty cream

1 teaspoon vanilla concentrate

1/4 cup sans sugar chocolate chips (discretionary)

Steps

1. Preheat oven to 350 degrees Fahrenheit.

2. Oil a doughnut container with spread or cooking splash.

3. In a bowl, whisk together the almond flour, sugar, baking powder, and salt.

4. Mix in the margarine, egg, cream, and vanilla concentrate until recently consolidated.

5. Crease in the chocolate chips, if utilizing.

6. Empty the hitter into the pre-arranged doughnut skillet and heat for 10-12 minutes, or until a toothpick embedded into the middle comes out clean.

Details and tips

For a more extravagant flavor, utilize dim cocoa powder.

Allow the donuts to cool totally prior to frosting and serving.

You can likewise make a keto doughnut glaze by combining as one 1/4 cup of powdered sugar, 1 tablespoon of weighty cream, and 1 teaspoon of vanilla concentrate.

Cooking time and temperature

Oven : 350 degrees Fahrenheit, 10-12 minutes

Visual cues

The donuts will be golden brown outwardly and cooked through within.

Nutritional info (per doughnut)

Calories: 150

Fat: 12 grams

Protein: 5 grams

Net carbs: 3 grams

<u>9. Keto Tiramisu</u>

Ingredients

1 cup weighty cream

1/4 cup granulated sugar

1/4 teaspoon vanilla concentrate

1/2 cup without sugar ladyfingers

1/4 cup without sugar cocoa powder

2 tablespoons espresso, solid or coffee, cooled

Steps

1. In a bowl, whip together the weighty cream, sugar, and vanilla concentrate until delicate pinnacles structure.

2. Plunge the ladyfingers in the espresso and organize them in a solitary layer in a 9x13 inch baking dish.

3. Spread portion of the whipped cream over the ladyfingers.

4. Sprinkle with half of the cocoa powder.

5. Rehash layers.

6. Cover and refrigerate for something like 4 hours prior to serving.

Details and tips

You can likewise utilize keto-accommodating ladyfingers, for example, those made with almond flour.

To make a keto espresso, brew espresso to the surprise of no one and afterward add 1/4 cup of weighty cream and 1/4 cup of granulated sugar.

To make a keto chocolate ganache, heat 1/2 cup of weighty cream in a pan over medium intensity until it simply starts to stew. Eliminate from the intensity and add 1/4 cup of unsweetened cocoa powder. Mix until smooth.

10. Keto Panna Cotta

Ingredients

1 cup weighty cream

1/4 cup granulated sugar

1/4 teaspoon vanilla concentrate

1/4 cup gelatin powder

1/4 cup cold water

1/4 cup sans sugar berries, for decorate (discretionary)

Steps

1. In a pan, heat the weighty cream, sugar, and vanilla concentrate over medium intensity until the sugar is broken down.

2. In a little bowl, whisk together the gelatin powder and cold water. Let represent 5 minutes, or until the gelatin is relaxed.

3. Mix the gelatin blend into the hot cream combination.

4. Empty the combination into ramekins or little glasses.

5. Refrigerate for somewhere around 4 hours, or until set.

6. Embellish with sans sugar berries, whenever wanted.

Details and tips

You can likewise utilize other keto-accommodating fruits in your panna cotta, like raspberries, strawberries, or blueberries.

To make a keto panna cotta with espresso, add 1/4 cup areas of strength for of to the hot cream combination.

11. Keto Fruit Salad

Ingredients

1 cup blended berries, new or frozen

1/4 cup unsweetened coconut chips

1/4 cup hacked nuts, like almonds or pecans

1 tablespoon granulated sugar

1/4 teaspoon vanilla concentrate

Steps

1. In a bowl, consolidate the berries, coconut drops, nuts, sugar, and vanilla concentrate.

2. Toss to coat.

Details and tips

You can involve any sort of berries that you like in your fruit salad.

To make a keto fruit salad with yogurt, add 1/2 cup of keto-accommodating yogurt to the bowl.

To make a keto fruit salad with whipped cream, add 1/4 cup of whipped cream to the bowl.

12. Keto Fudge

Ingredients

1 cup weighty cream

1/4 cup granulated sugar

1/4 teaspoon vanilla concentrate

1/4 cup unsweetened cocoa powder

Steps

1. In a pan, heat the weighty cream, sugar, and vanilla concentrate over

medium intensity until the sugar is broken down.

2. Remove from the heat and mix in the cocoa powder.

3. Empty the blend into a little dish and let cool totally.

4. Cut into squares and serve.

Chapter 10

Keto Fish and seafood Recipes

1. Salmon with Creamy Dill Sauce

Ingredients

1 (4-ounce) salmon filet

1 tablespoon olive oil

1 teaspoon salt

1/2 teaspoon dark pepper

1/4 cup harsh cream

1/4 cup mayonnaise

2 tablespoons new dill, slashed

1 tablespoon lemon juice

Steps

1. Preheat stove to 400 degrees F (200 degrees C).

2. Season salmon with olive oil, salt, and pepper.

3. Place salmon in a baking dish and prepare for 15-20 minutes, or until

cooked through.

4. While salmon is cooking, whisk together acrid cream, mayonnaise, dill, and lemon juice.

5. Serve salmon with creamy dill sauce.

Details and Tips

You can involve any sort of salmon for this recipe.

On the off chance that you don't have new dill, you can utilize dried dill.

Serve the salmon with your most loved keto-accommodating sides, for example, roasted vegetables or cauliflower rice.

Cooking Times and Temperatures

Preheat broiler to 400 degrees F (200 degrees C).

Heat salmon for 15-20 minutes, or until cooked through.

Visual cue

The salmon ought to be cooked through and flaky.

The creamy dill sauce ought to be smooth and creamy.

Nutritional Info

Calories: 280

Absolute Fat: 20 grams

Soaked Fat: 3 grams

Cholesterol: 85 milligrams

Sodium: 250 milligrams

Starches: 2 grams

Fiber: 1 gram

Sugar: 1 gram

Protein: 20 grams

2. Salmon With Bacon and Tomato Cream Sauce

Ingredients

1 (4-ounce) salmon filet

1 tablespoon olive oil

1/2 teaspoon salt

1/4 teaspoon dark pepper

1/4 cup bacon bits

1/4 cup weighty cream

1/4 cup tomato sauce

1 tablespoon new basil, slashed

Steps

1. Preheat broiler to 400 degrees F (200 degrees C).

2. Season salmon with olive oil, salt, and pepper.

3. Place salmon in a baking dish and top with bacon bits.

4. In a little bowl, whisk together weighty cream, tomato sauce, and basil.

5. Pour cream sauce over salmon.

6. Heat for 15-20 minutes, or until salmon is cooked through.

Details and Tips

You can involve any kind of salmon for this recipe.

In the event that you don't have bacon bits, you can utilize cooked bacon, disintegrated.

Serve the salmon with your most loved keto-accommodating sides, for example, roasted vegetables or cauliflower rice.

Cooking Times and Temperatures

Preheat broiler to 400 degrees F (200 degrees C).

Heat salmon for 15-20 minutes, or until cooked through.

Visual cue

The salmon ought to be cooked through and flaky.

The bacon ought to be fresh.

The cream sauce ought to be smooth and creamy.

Nutritional Info

Calories: 300

Fat: 25 grams

Soaked Fat: 9 grams

Cholesterol: 85 milligrams

Sodium: 250 milligrams

Sugars: 5 grams

Fiber: 1 gram

Sugar: 1 gram

Protein: 20 grams

3. Avocado and Basil Salmon

Ingredients

1 (4-ounce) salmon filet

1 tablespoon olive oil

1/2 teaspoon salt

1/4 teaspoon dark pepper

1/2 avocado, pounded

1/4 cup new basil, slashed

1 tablespoon lemon juice

Steps

1. Preheat stove to 400 degrees F (200 degrees C).

2. Season salmon with olive oil, salt, and pepper.

3. Place salmon in a baking dish and top with avocado, basil, and lemon juice.

4. Prepare for 15-20 minutes, or until salmon

5. Heat for 15-20 minutes, or until salmon is cooked through.

6. Serve right away.

Details and tips

You can involve any sort of salmon for this recipe.

In the event that you don't have new basil, you can utilize dried basil.

To make the avocado garnish, just pound the avocado with a fork until smooth.

You can likewise add different garnishes to the salmon, like slashed tomatoes, red onion, or escapades.

Nutritional information

Calories: 300

Fat: 25 grams

Immersed Fat: 4 grams

Cholesterol: 85 milligrams

Sodium: 250 milligrams

Sugars: 5 grams

Fiber: 2 grams

Sugar: 1 gram

Protein: 20 grams

4. Keto Salmon Cakes

Ingredients

1 (15-ounce) can salmon, depleted and chipped

1/2 cup almond flour

1/4 cup ground Parmesan cheddar

1 egg, beaten

1 tablespoon olive oil

1/2 teaspoon salt

1/4 teaspoon dark pepper

Steps

1. Preheat oven to 400 degrees F (200 degrees C).

2. In a bowl, join salmon, almond flour, Parmesan cheddar, egg, olive oil, salt, and pepper.

3. Blend well until joined.

4. Structure the combination into patties.

5. Heat for 15-20 minutes, or until cooked through.

Details and Tips

You can involve any kind of salmon for this recipe.

In the event that you don't have almond flour, you can utilize coconut flour or another without gluten flour.

Serve the salmon cakes with your most loved keto-accommodating plunging sauce, for example, harsh cream or tartar sauce.

Cooking Times and Temperatures

Preheat oven to 400 degrees F (200 degrees C).

Heat salmon cakes for 15-20 minutes, or until cooked through.

Visual cue

The salmon cakes ought to be golden brown and cooked through.

Nutritional Info

Calories: 250

Absolute Fat: 20 grams

Immersed Fat: 4 grams

Cholesterol: 85 milligrams

Sodium: 250 milligrams

Carbohydrates: 5 grams

Fiber: 2 grams

Sugar: 1 gram

Protein: 20 grams

5. Salmon and Asparagus Foil Packs

Ingredients:

1 (4-ounce) salmon filet

1 pound asparagus, managed

1 tablespoon olive oil

1/2 teaspoon salt

1/4 teaspoon dark pepper

1/4 cup lemon juice

Steps

1. Preheat stove to 400 degrees F (200 degrees C).

2. Line a baking sheet with material paper.

3. Place salmon filet in the focal point of the material paper.

4. Encompass the salmon with asparagus.

5. Shower with olive oil, salt, pepper, and lemon juice.

6. Crease the material paper over the salmon and asparagus to make a bundle.

7. Prepare for 15-20 minutes, or until salmon is cooked through.

Details and Tips

You can involve any sort of salmon for this recipe.

On the off chance that you don't have asparagus, you can utilize different vegetables, like broccoli, zucchini, or carrots.

You can likewise add different flavors to the salmon, for example, garlic powder, onion powder, or paprika.

Cooking Times and Temperatures

Preheat oven to 400 degrees F (200 degrees C).

Prepare salmon for 15-20 minutes, or until cooked through.

Visual cue

The salmon ought to be cooked through and flaky.

The asparagus ought to be delicate.

Nutritional Info

Calories: 300

Fat: 25 grams

Immersed Fat: 4 grams

Cholesterol: 85 milligrams

Sodium: 250 milligrams

Sugars: 5 grams

Fiber: 2 grams

Sugar: 1 gram

Protein: 20 grams

6. Keto Salmon With Tzatziki Sauce

Ingredients

1 (4-ounce) salmon filet

1 tablespoon olive oil

1/2 teaspoon salt

1/4 teaspoon dark pepper

1 cup tzatziki sauce

Steps

1. Preheat oven to 400 degrees F (200 degrees C).

2. Season salmon with olive oil, salt, and pepper.

3. Place salmon in a baking dish and top with tzatziki sauce.

4. Heat for 15-20 minutes, or until salmon is cooked through.

Details and Tips

You can involve any kind of salmon for this recipe.

On the off chance that you don't have tzatziki sauce, you can make your own by consolidating Greek yogurt, cucumber, dill, garlic, lemon squeeze, and salt.

5. Serve the salmon quickly with the tzatziki sauce.

Details and tips

You can likewise barbecue or sear the salmon as opposed to baking it.

In the event that you are barbecuing the salmon, brush it with olive oil prior to barbecuing.

In the event that you are searing the salmon, cook it over medium intensity for 3-4 minutes for every side, or until cooked through.

Nutritional information

Calories: 400

Whole Fat: 30 grams

Soaked Fat: 5 grams

Cholesterol: 85 milligrams

Sodium: 250 milligrams

Carbs: 5 grams

 Fiber: 2 grams

 Sugar: 1 gram

Protein: 20 grams

7. Salmon Stuffed Avocado

Ingredients

 1 ready avocado, divided and pitted

 1 (4-ounce) salmon filet, cooked and chipped

 1/4 cup hacked red onion

 1/4 cup hacked tomato

 1 tablespoon hacked new cilantro

 1/2 teaspoon salt

 1/4 teaspoon dark pepper

Steps

1. Scoop out the flesh of the avocado, leaving a dainty layer of flesh on the base and sides.

2. In a bowl, join the salmon, red onion, tomato, cilantro, salt, and pepper.

3. Spoon the salmon combination into the avocado shells.

4. Serve right away.

Details and Tips

You can involve any kind of salmon for this recipe.

In the event that you don't have cilantro, you can utilize parsley or another spice.

You can likewise add different fixings to the avocado, like destroyed cheddar or diced cucumber.

Cooking Times and Temperatures

No cooking required.

Visual cue

The avocado ought to be ready and delicate.

The salmon combination ought to be equally appropriated in the avocado shells.

Nutritional Info

Calories: 300

Whole Fat: 25 grams

Immersed Fat: 4 grams

Cholesterol: 85 milligrams

Sodium: 250 milligrams

Carbs: 5 grams

Fiber: 2 grams

Sugar: 1 gram

Protein: 20 grams

8. Keto Sushi Rolls

Ingredients

1 (8-ounce) bundle of nori sheets

1/2 cup cooked sushi rice

1/4 cup cucumber, daintily cut

1/4 cup avocado, daintily cut

1/4 cup impersonation crab, destroyed

1 tablespoon mayonnaise

1 teaspoon Sriracha sauce

Steps

1. Spread the sushi rice equally over a nori sheet.

2. Top with cucumber, avocado, impersonation crab, mayonnaise, and Sriracha sauce.

3. Roll up the nori sheet firmly.

4. Cut the roll into 6-8 pieces.

Details and Tips

You can involve any sort of sushi rice for this recipe.

 On the off chance that you don't have impersonation crab, you can utilize cooked shrimp or fish.

You can likewise add different fixings to the sushi rolls, like cured ginger, wasabi, or sesame seeds.

Cooking Times and Temperatures

 No cooking required.

Visual cue

The sushi rolls ought to be firmly rolled.

The cuts ought to be uniformly cut.

Nutritional Info

Calories: 300

Absolute Fat: 25 grams

Immersed Fat: 4 grams

Cholesterol: 85 milligrams

Sodium: 250 milligrams

Starches: 5 grams

Fiber: 2 grams

Sugar: 1 gram

Protein: 20 grams

9. Keto Salmon Tartare

Ingredients

1 (4-ounce) salmon filet, cooked and chipped

1/4 cup mayonnaise

1 tablespoon Dijon mustard

1 tablespoon tricks, depleted

1 tablespoon hacked new dill

1/2 teaspoon salt

1/4 teaspoon dark pepper

Steps

1. In a bowl, consolidate salmon, mayonnaise, Dijon mustard, escapades, dill, salt, and pepper.

2. Blend well until consolidated.

3. Serve promptly with saltines or vegetables.

Details and Tips

You can involve any sort of salmon for this recipe.

In the event that you don't have Dijon mustard, you can utilize one more kind of mustard.

You can likewise add different ingredients to the tartare, like cleaved onions, celery, or cucumbers.

Cooking Times and Temperatures

No cooking required.

Visual Cues

The salmon ought to be chipped.

The tartare ought to be equitably blended.

Nutritional Info

Calories: 250

Complete Fat: 20 grams

Immersed Fat: 4 grams

Cholesterol: 85 milligrams

Sodium: 250 milligrams

Carbs: 5 grams

Fiber: 2 grams

Sugar: 1 gram

Protein: 20 grams

10. Walnut Crusted Salmon

Ingredients

1 (4-ounce) salmon filet

1 tablespoon olive oil

1/2 teaspoon salt

1/4 teaspoon dark pepper

1/4 cup walnuts, slashed

1 tablespoon Parmesan cheddar

1 tablespoon slashed new dill

Steps

1. Preheat broiler to 400 degrees F (200 degrees C).

2. Season salmon with olive oil, salt, and pepper.

3. In a little bowl, join walnuts, Parmesan cheddar, and dill.

4. Compress the walnut blend onto the salmon filet.

5. Prepare for 15-20 minutes, or until salmon is cooked through.

Details and tips

You can involve any sort of salmon for this recipe.

 On the off chance that you don't have walnuts, you can utilize almonds or walnuts.

You can likewise add different garnishes to the salmon, like destroyed cheddar or diced vegetables.

Cooking Times and Temperatures

Preheat oven to 400 degrees F (200 degrees C).

Prepare salmon for 15-20 minutes, or until cooked through.

Visual Cues

The salmon ought to be cooked through and flaky.

The walnut hull ought to be golden brown and fresh.

Nutritional Info

 Calories: 300

 Whole Fat: 25 grams

 Immersed Fat: 4 grams

 Cholesterol: 85 milligrams

 Sodium: 250 milligrams

 Sugars: 5 grams

 Fiber: 2 grams

 Sugar: 1 gram

 Protein: 20 grams

Chapter 11

Keto Poultry Recipes

1. Creamy Tuscan Chicken

Ingredients

1 pound boneless, skinless chicken bosoms or thighs, cut into 1-inch pieces

1 tablespoon olive oil

1/2 cup slashed onion

2 cloves garlic, minced

1 (14.5 ounce) can diced tomatoes, undrained

1 (10.75 ounce) can dense cream of mushroom soup

1/2 cup ground Parmesan cheese

1/4 teaspoon dried thyme

1/4 teaspoon salt

1/8 teaspoon dark pepper

Step

1. Heat the olive oil in a huge skillet over medium intensity. Add the chicken and cook until seared on all sides.

2. Mix in the onion and garlic and cook until mellowed.

3. Add the diced tomatoes, cream of mushroom soup, Parmesan cheese, thyme, salt, and pepper. Bring to a stew and cook for 10 minutes, or until the chicken is cooked through.

4. Serve right away.

Visual cue

The chicken ought to be cooked through and the sauce ought to be thickened.

Nutritional info (per serving)

Calories: 380

Fat: 25 grams

Protein: 30 grams

Net carbs: 5 grams

2. Cheese and Spinach Stuffed Chicken

Ingredients

4 boneless, skinless chicken bosoms

1/2 cup destroyed Parmesan cheese

1/2 cup cleaved spinach

1/4 cup cleaved onion

2 cloves garlic, minced

1/4 teaspoon salt

1/8 teaspoon dark pepper

Step

1. Preheat oven to 375 degrees F (190 degrees C).

2. Pound the chicken bosoms to 1/2-inch thickness.

3. In a medium bowl, consolidate the Parmesan cheese, spinach, onion, garlic, salt, and pepper.

4. Spread the cheese blend equally over the chicken bosoms.

5. Roll up the chicken bosoms and secure with toothpicks.

6. Place the chicken rolls in a baking dish and prepare for 30 minutes, or until the chicken is cooked through.

Visual cue

The chicken ought to be cooked through and the cheese ought to be softened and effervescent.

Nutritional info (per serving)

Calories: 350

Fat: 25 grams

Protein: 30 grams

Net carbs: 5 grams

3. Buffalo Chicken Soup

Ingredients

1 pound boneless, skinless chicken bosoms, cooked and destroyed

1 (14.5 ounce) can chicken stock

1 (10.75 ounce) can consolidated cream of chicken soup

1/2 cup hot sauce

1/4 cup ground Parmesan cheese

1/4 teaspoon salt

1/8 teaspoon dark pepper

Step

1. In a huge pot, consolidate the chicken stock, cream of chicken soup, hot sauce, Parmesan cheese, salt, and pepper. Bring to a stew over medium intensity.

2. Mix in the chipped chicken and cook for 5 minutes, or until warmed through.

Visual cue

The soup ought to be hot and the chicken ought to be warmed through.

Nutritional info (per serving)

Calories: 300

Fat: 20 grams

Protein: 20 grams

Net carbs: 5 grams

4. Keto Chicken Enchilada Bowl

Ingredients

1 pound boneless, skinless chicken bosoms, cooked and destroyed

1 (10 ounce) could enchilada at any point sauce

1 (10 ounce) can diced tomatoes and green chilies, undrained

1 cup destroyed Cheddar cheese

1/2 cup slashed cilantro

1/4 teaspoon salt

1/8 teaspoon dark pepper

Step

1. In an enormous bowl, consolidate the chicken, enchilada sauce, diced tomatoes and green chilies, Cheddar cheese, cilantro, salt, and pepper.

2. Serve in bowls and appreciate.

Visual cue

The chicken ought to be cooked through. The bowl ought to be loaded with chicken, enchilada sauce, cheese, and cilantro.

Nutritional info (per serving)

Calories: 400

Fat: 30 grams

Protein: 30 grams

Net carbs: 10 grams

5. Sheet Pan Chicken and Rainbow Veggies

Ingredients

1 pound boneless, skinless chicken bosoms or thighs, managed

1 tablespoon olive oil

1/2 teaspoon salt

1/4 teaspoon dark pepper

1 (10 ounce) pack frozen broccoli florets

1 (10 ounce) pack frozen carrots, cut

1/2 cup slashed red onion

1/4 cup slashed new parsley

Step

1. Preheat oven to 400 degrees F (200 degrees C).

2. Throw the chicken with the olive oil, salt, and pepper.

3. Spread the chicken in a solitary layer on a baking sheet.

4. Add the broccoli, carrots, and onion to the baking sheet.

5. Heat for 25-30 minutes, or until the chicken is cooked through and the vegetables are delicate.

6. Sprinkle with parsley and serve.

Visual cue

The chicken ought to be cooked through and the vegetables ought to be delicate.

Nutritional info (per serving)

Calories: 300

Fat: 15 grams

Protein: 30 grams

 Net carbs: 5 grams

<u>Tips</u>

 For a more tasty chicken, marinate it in your most loved keto-accommodating marinade for something like 30 minutes prior to cooking.

 You can likewise add different vegetables to the sheet pan, like zucchini, squash, or ringer peppers.

 To make this recipe early, you can cook the chicken and vegetables independently and then, later, gather the dish not long prior to serving.

Chapter 12

Keto Beef, Lamb and Pork Recipes

1. Stuffed Bell Peppers

Ingredients

2 enormous bell peppers, split and deseeded

1 pound ground beef

1/2 onion, slashed

1/2 cup ground Parmesan cheddar

1/4 cup slashed new parsley

1/4 teaspoon salt

1/8 teaspoon dark pepper

Steps

1. Preheat oven to 375 degrees F (190 degrees C).

2. In an enormous skillet, brown the ground beef over medium intensity. Channel off any abundance fat.

3. Stir in the onion and cook until relaxed.

4. Stir in the Parmesan cheddar, parsley, salt, and pepper.

5. Spoon the beef combination into the pre-arranged bell peppers.

6. Prepare in the preheated stove for 20-25 minutes, or until the peppers are delicate.

Details and tips

For a veggie lover choice, use ground turkey or tofu rather than ground beef.

You can likewise add different vegetables to the filling, like diced carrots, zucchini, or mushrooms.

Present with a side of cauliflower rice or simmered vegetables.

Visual cue

The stuffed bell peppers ought to be golden brown and the filling ought to be cooked through.

Nutritional information (per serving)

Calories: 300

Fat: 18 grams

Protein: 20 grams

Sugars: 10 grams

2. Keto Meatballs

Ingredients

1 pound ground beef

1/2 cup ground Parmesan cheddar

1/4 cup almond flour

1/4 cup slashed new parsley

1 egg, beaten

1 teaspoon salt

1/2 teaspoon dark pepper

Steps

1. Preheat oven to 400 degrees F (200 degrees C).

2. In an enormous bowl, consolidate the ingredients as a whole.

3. Blend well until uniformly joined.

4. Structure the combination into meatballs.

5. Put the meatballs on a baking sheet fixed with material paper.

6. Heat in the preheated broiler for 15-20 minutes, or until cooked through.

Details and tips

You can likewise add different ingredients to the meatballs, like diced

onion, garlic, or breadcrumbs.

 Serve the meatballs with your most loved plunging sauce, for example, marinara sauce or ketchup.

Visual cue

The meatballs ought to be golden brown and cooked through.

Nutritional information (per serving)

Calories: 250

Fat: 20 grams

 Protein: 15 grams

Carbohydrates: 5 grams

3. Bacon-Wrapped Pork Tenderloin

Ingredients

1 (1-pound) pork tenderloin, managed

 12 cuts bacon

 1 teaspoon salt

 1/2 teaspoon dark pepper

Steps

1. Preheat oven to 400 degrees F (200 degrees C).

2. Wrap the pork tenderloin with the bacon cuts, covering on a case by case basis.

3. Season with salt and pepper.

4. Place the pork tenderloin in a baking dish.

5. Prepare in the preheated broiler for 30-35 minutes, or until the pork is cooked through and the bacon is fresh.

Details and tips

You can likewise utilize chicken or turkey tenderloin rather than pork tenderloin.

Serve the pork tenderloin with your #1 sides, like cooked vegetables or pureed potatoes.

Visual cue

The pork tenderloin ought to be cooked through and the bacon ought to be fresh.

Nutritional information (per serving)

Calories: 450

Fat: 30 grams

Protein: 30 grams

Sugars: 5 grams

4. Beef Stir-Fry

Ingredients

1 pound beef sirloin, meagerly cut

1 tablespoon olive oil

1 onion, slashed

2 cloves garlic, minced

1 red bell pepper, slashed

1 green bell pepper, slashed

1 (14.5 ounce) can diced tomatoes, undrained

1 (10 ounce) can beef stock

1 tablespoon soy sauce

1 teaspoon ground ginger

1/2 teaspoon dark pepper

1/4 cup cleaved new cilantro

Steps

1. Heat the olive oil in an enormous skillet or wok over medium-high

intensity.

2. Add the beef and cook until sautéed.

3. Add the onion and garlic and cook until relaxed.

4. Add the bell peppers and cook for 2-3 minutes, or until relaxed.

5. Stir in the diced tomatoes, beef stock, soy sauce, ginger, and dark pepper.

6. Bring to a stew and cook for 10-15 minutes, or until the sauce has thickened.

7. Stir in the cilantro and serve right away.

Details and tips

You can likewise utilize different kinds of beef, for example, flank steak or sirloin tips.

In the event that you don't have a wok, you can utilize an enormous skillet.

Serve the stir-fry with cauliflower rice or noodles.

Visual cue

The beef stir-fry ought to be cooked through and the vegetables ought to be delicate.

Nutritional information (per serving)

Calories: 350

Fat: 20 grams

Protein: 25 grams

Sugars: 10 grams

5. Lamb Curry

Ingredients

1 pound lamb shoulder, cut into blocks

1 tablespoon olive oil

1 onion, slashed

2 cloves garlic, minced

1 (1-inch) piece ginger, stripped and minced

1 teaspoon ground cumin

1 teaspoon ground coriander

1/2 teaspoon turmeric powder

1/2 teaspoon garam masala

1/2 teaspoon cayenne pepper

1 (14.5 ounce) can diced tomatoes, undrained

1 (10 ounce) can beef stock

1/2 cup weighty cream

Salt and pepper to taste

Steps

1. Heat the olive oil in an enormous skillet or Dutch broiler over medium intensity.

2. Add the lamb and cook until sautéed on all sides.

3. Add the onion, garlic, ginger, cumin, coriander, turmeric, garam masala, and cayenne pepper and cook for 1 moment, or until fragrant.

4. Stir in the diced tomatoes, beef stock, and weighty cream.

5. Bring to a stew and cook for 30 minutes, or until the lamb is delicate.

6. Season with salt and pepper to taste.

Details and tips

You can likewise utilize different cuts of lamb, for example, leg of lamb or shoulder cleaves.

.On the off chance that you don't have a Dutch broiler, you can utilize an enormous pot.

Serve the lamb curry with rice or naan bread.

Visual cue

The lamb curry ought to be cooked through and the sauce ought to be

thickened.

Nutritional information (per serving)

Calories: 500

Fat: 30 grams

Protein: 35 grams

Carbohydrates: 10 grams

Chapter 13

<u>100 Keto Recipes</u>

<u>Breakfast</u>

1. Keto Pancakes with Sugar-Free Syrup

2. Bacon and Cheese Egg Muffins

3. Avocado Breakfast Bowl

4. Sausage and Spinach Frittata

5. Almond Flour Waffles

6. Chia Seed Pudding with Berries

7. Creamy Keto Coffee Smoothie

8. Smoked Salmon and Cream Cheese Roll-Ups

9. Greek Yogurt Parfait with Nuts and Berries

10. Keto Breakfast Burrito with Cauliflower Tortilla

<u>Lunch</u>

11. Caesar Salad with Grilled Chicken

12. Avocado Tuna Salad Lettuce Wraps

13. Broccoli and Cheddar Soup

14. Cobb Salad with Bacon and Avocado

15. Keto Sushi Rolls with Cucumber Wrapper

16. Turkey and Cheese Roll-Ups

17. Zucchini Noodles with Pesto and Grilled Chicken

18. Creamy Cauliflower Soup

19. Egg Salad Stuffed Avocado

20. Keto-friendly Bento Box with Cheese, Nuts, and Berries

Dinner

21. Grilled Steak with Garlic Butter

22. Garlic Parmesan Baked Chicken Wings

23. Spaghetti Squash with Meatballs and Marinara Sauce

24. Lemon Herb Grilled Fish

25. Keto Beef Stir-Fry with Veggies

26. Creamy Garlic Parmesan Shrimp

27. Stuffed Bell Peppers with Ground Turkey and Cheese

28. Cabbage Noodle Beef Stroganoff

29. Baked Salmon with Asparagus

30. Chicken Alfredo with Zucchini Noodles

Snacks

31. Cheese Crisps

32. Guacamole with Veggie Sticks

33. Keto Trail Mix with Nuts and Seeds

34. Parmesan Crusted Zucchini Fries

35. Mini Pepper Nachos with Ground Beef

36. Deviled Eggs with Bacon

37. Buffalo Cauliflower Bites with Ranch Dip

38. Almond Butter Fat Bombs

39. Seaweed Snacks

40. Ham and Cream Cheese Roll-Ups

Desserts

41. Keto Chocolate Avocado Mousse

42. Berry Coconut Chia Popsicles

43. Peanut Butter Chocolate Fat Bombs

44. Keto Cheesecake Bites

45. Chocolate Peanut Butter Cups

46. Coconut Flour Chocolate Chip Cookies

47. Vanilla Almond Fat Bombs

48. Keto Lemon Bars

49. No-Bake Chocolate Coconut Bars

50. Mixed Berry Parfait with Whipped Cream

Sides

51. Cauliflower Rice

52. Creamed Spinach

53. Roasted Brussels Sprouts with Bacon

54. Loaded Cauliflower Mash

55. Cucumber Avocado Salad

56. Broccoli Salad with Bacon and Cheese

57. Garlic Parmesan Green Beans

58. Creamy Coleslaw

59. Cheesy Garlic Mashed Cauliflower

60. Stuffed Portobello Mushrooms

Breads and Wraps

61. Keto Cloud Bread

62. Almond Flour Tortillas

63. Lettuce Wraps with Chicken Salad

64. Coconut Flour Flatbread

65. Cheesy Garlic Breadsticks

66. Keto-Friendly Bagels

67. Spinach and Feta Wraps

68. Zucchini Bread

69. Cauliflower Crust Calzone

70. Flaxseed Wraps

Drinks

71. Keto Bulletproof Coffee

72. Matcha Latte with Almond Milk

73. Keto-friendly Green Smoothie

74. Strawberry Lemonade Slushie

75. Iced Coffee with Heavy Cream

76. Keto Hot Chocolate

77. Cucumber Mint Electrolyte Drink

78. Herbal Tea with MCT Oil

79. Sparkling Water with Lime

80. Keto-Friendly Protein Shake

International Cuisine

81. Keto Chicken Curry

82. Cauliflower Fried Rice

83. Keto Tacos with Lettuce Wraps

84. Thai Coconut Soup (Tom Kha Gai)

85. Keto Butter Chicken

86. Greek Salad with Feta and Olives

87. Italian Zucchini Noodles with Pesto

88. Mexican Cauliflower Rice Bowl

89. Keto Pad Thai with Shirataki Noodles

90. Japanese-inspired Sashimi Salad

Party and Gatherings Recipes

91. Bacon-Wrapped Jalapeno Poppers

Printed in Great Britain
by Amazon

be51385f-e313-4038-8412-c8f814e9b4baR01